CAR WARS

Battles on the Road to Nowhere

Chris Mosey

© 2000 Chris Mosey
ISBN: 1-901250-40-7

VISION Paperbacks
20 Queen Anne Street
London W1M 0AY
UK
email: sheenadewan@compuserve.com
website: http://www.visionpaperbacks.demon.co.uk

Publisher: Sheena Dewan
Cover image: © 2000 Nickolai Globe
Layout: Justine Hounam

Printed and bound in Great Britain by
Biddles Ltd, www.biddles.co.uk

Dedication

For those who fought them

Acknowledgements

I would like to thank everyone who helped me in the research and writing of this book: Reclaim the Streets for giving me the initial idea; Rodney Dale, David Henshaw, Wolfgang Zuckermann, Veronique Charpenet, John Tyme, Roger Higman, Barbara Bryant, Derek Wall, Linda Beard, Andy Castellano Smith and Tom Williams for sparing me their time; the people I talked to on the streets of Cambridge; my partner Jean Hudson for putting up with me during the writing and who still swears the coach hit "a ton" on that school outing along the Preston bypass all those years ago; Lion Television, whose production of *The Road to Nowhere* for BBC 2 gave me an excellent overview of motorway construction and road protest in Britain and Jason, the plumber, who taped the programme for me; Sally Snow and Paul Kingsnorth at The Ecologist; the staff at both university and public libraries in Cambridge for their help in locating relevant newspaper articles; all whose written work and ideas I have so shamelessly plundered; and finally at Vision Sheena Dewan who commissioned the book and Caroline Jory, my editor, who so valiantly saw it through to completion.

By the same author:

Cruel Awakening – Sweden and the Killing of Olof Palme,
Christopher Hurst, London, St. Martin's Press, New York,
1991.

*The Magic Horse – 'Devil's plaything' that became a national
symbol*, Boox, Stockholm, 1999.

About the Author:

For 11 years, Chris Mosey worked as a correspondent in Sweden for *The Times* and the *Observer*. He has also contributed to a variety of international magazines.

Chris currently lives in Cambridge where, like a great many other people, he rides a bicycle.

Contents

INTRODUCTION

The car and the problems it causes in the modern world are symptoms of a deep sickness in our civilisation. They are portents of a fast gathering environmental holocaust we are bringing upon ourselves. Most of us are aware that something is wrong yet desperately try to hide from that awareness, to push it out of our minds, as we get on with day-to-day survival. As a species, we humans have never been too good at dealing with the long term. The economist Maynard Keynes was fond of saying that there was no such thing as the long term because in the long term "we are all dead"[1]

True enough. Our children, on the other hand, will be alive.

We like to think of ourselves as good, responsible people and loving parents. So we hold United Nations' conferences, set up environmental 'think tanks' and pass cosmetic legislation. But basically it is business as usual: our polluting, voracious consumer societies stay the same. We continue to use up natural resources and change our environment for the worse. Cars keep pouring off production lines and onto already overcrowded roads. It is just that in the third millennium, at the same time as all of this is going on, we delude ourselves that we have initiated a 'green revolution'. We imagine that we have got it under control. We think that if we segregate our garbage and recycle a few bottles and newspapers, the holocaust will not happen.

We are always on the move, which is why cars are so important to us. We are possessed of a neurotic restlessness in which we are forever travelling in hope, only rarely arriving to exist in the here and now. When you are heading somewhere marvellous – the goal of a seemingly inexorable force we call 'progress' – then faults in the present are excusable. Alexander

Pope summed it up more than 300 years ago:

> *Hope springs eternal in the human breast*
> *Man never Is, but always To be blest.*

But Pope also said:

> *The learn'd is happy nature to explore*
> *The fool is happy that he knows no more.*[2]

There are some questions we should perhaps be asking ourselves. Is it progress simply to do something, to get somewhere ever faster? Just where are we going – is progress really bringing about a better world, or are we merely being pulled blindly in its wake?

Mahatma Ghandi once said, "There's more to life than increasing its speed."

Roads choked with cars? People in turn choking on the pollution they produce? "Ah well, that's progress, isn't it?" It is a pretty standard riposte when the subject is broached. To which there are two replies: Is such a situation truly progress? And – if it is – do we want it?

One of the basic premises of this book, is that the problems caused by the car are more acute in Britain than elsewhere in the western world and that it is here that they will have to be dealt with first. Other countries have the same problem, but they also have more space, which allows the ravages of so-called progress to be less visible. In crowded Britain, the blight on cities and countryside caused by the automobile and road-building is only too apparent. All that is needed to bring this home, apart from the appalling quality of the air we breathe in our cities, is the sight of Twyford Down the once majestic chalk upland that formed a backdrop to the ancient city of Winchester, vandalised beyond repair by the M3 motorway. Yet as the blight of the car and road building has settled on 'this sceptr'd isle', as the bulldozers have moved in, the vast majority of the population – just as they did in the Blitz – muddle through, content with the odd whinge of complaint. "You get there faster," they croak. "It's progress, isn't it?"

Progress where? Into the ecological shredder? Cars, as a

problem – more and more of them flooding onto choked up roads, using up dwindling oil reserves, contributing to pollution and global warming – are part and parcel of a far greater problem: that long, lingering, perhaps terminal blight that will soon fall upon us as a species if we do not change our ways. The likelihood now is that humanity will go out not with the bang we feared in the Cold War era but with a last sad, despairing cough and an elongated, asthmatic gasp of "Well, it's progress, isn't it?"

Progress is presently leading us towards a global economy. This, our leaders tell us, will be our salvation. Yet a global economy without global government can only accelerate our destruction of the planet. It grants multi-national companies the *de facto* right to ride roughshod over environmental concerns, which usually start at a very local level, and to set countries like China and India travelling down the same road that we in the West are just beginning to realise actually leads nowhere.

Behind these physical problems, there is an even greater problem which is philosophical in nature. This concerns the way we see our world and our place in the universe. The car is admittedly a small, yet very visible part of these other massive problems now hovering over the heads of our children. The car is something we could actually do something about – if the will was there, which at the time of writing it manifestly is not.

And who am I to be banging on like this? The answer is a hack journalist who, having lived a large part of his life elsewhere – in Sweden and France – returned in 1995 to Britain. I wound up in the ancient university city of Cambridge. Here I settled, travelled about and found that, despite its many failings, Britain was not as bad as I had often imagined it from a distance. I liked the general mateyness of the people (as opposed to what I had experienced – generalising horrendously – as the shy aloofness of the Swedes and the self-obsessed arrogance of the French).

The street where I lived was in Romsey Town, on the 'wrong' side of the tracks. Romsey has a very mixed population: in addition to those who were born there, you now find Poles and Italians who moved in during the war, Jamaicans who arrived in the 1950s, academics unable to find accommodation in more fashionable parts of the city, and people who work in the burgeoning computer software and micro-electronics industries. And at the end of the street was a meeting place, something you yearn for when you live abroad, The Pub – a warm, friendly place of refuge.

But no matter how I adapted and tried to fit in to modern Britain, I remained appalled by the degree of despoilation of town and country that had taken place during the period I had been away. A time when, according to tabloid newspaper lore, Mrs Thatcher had turned Britain around and made it Great again. If that was the case, I thought, it certainly did not look great. It did not smell great either. Apart from the sheer ugliness of its cities and its urban sprawl, the most visible evidence of this despoilation was the pollution and the numbers of cars and trucks on the roads.

Cambridge has a population of 110,000 and another 250,000 people living within a 15 mile radius. Some 125,000 car trips are made in and out of the city daily, 40 per cent of them during the morning and evening rush hours. Traffic in the countryside around the city has doubled since 1981, and Government forecasts say it will continue to grow faster in the Cambridge area than anywhere else in Britain.[3] Mill Road, a main artery into the city centre at the top of my street, was clogged with traffic each morning, as people drove in to work; then again in the evening as they all went home again – in 90 per cent of cases, one person to a car.

Elsewhere I discovered motorways and multi-lane trunk roads criss-crossing the country, heaving under a constant neurotic pulse of traffic. I experienced the horror of the M25 London orbital motorway, which Mrs T had hailed as "a magnificent achievement". The country seemed to have shrunk alarmingly. I travelled down the M4 to Cornwall, which had seemed a distant, exotic place in my youth. Now that you could reach it so easily, that mystery had evaporated. Of course, it was not just the roads and the cars. Towns had lost their identity: they had the same stores selling the same things, the same supermarkets and shopping centres, the same advertising hoardings, the same ring roads and baffling, ugly plethora of road signs. People spoke 'estuary' English and talked about the same things – mostly what they had watched on television the night before or how 'their' football team was doing. They were losing their individuality, I decided, and the young seemed to be getting as stoned or drunk as possible to avoid thinking about the mess they would inherit. Was I being objective? It is always difficult to work such things out. Maybe I had just grown old, grouchy and disillusioned while I had been away. Maybe it was six of one, half a dozen of the other. But maybe Britons instead of never, never being slaves had simply closed their eyes and accepted a worsening of their world, as it had been wrecked by the car.

However, it is time to give some credit where it is due. Cambridge, where I settled, has actually made some attempts to deal with the car problem. Brian Smith, Director of Environment and Transport for Cambridgeshire County Council, says, "Our strategy of removing through traffic from the city centre is working. It may have taken a while for some people to accept the need for it but it frees up road space for essential users."[4] However, traffic entering the outskirts was up 30 per cent in 1999 and with continuing economic and population growth, is expected to get even worse. Public transport is appalling. Buses are expensive and rarely run to time, despite special bus lanes – though the city's Park & Ride scheme is hailed as a great success, with more than 750,000 trips a year.[5] Being flat, Cambridge naturally attracts vast numbers of cyclists and a great many bike lanes have been created to accommodate them. However, whilst I enjoy cycling – after my European experience – I was rather put out by what I saw at the time as an example of famous British 'muddling through' when it came to these bike lanes. At best they had a habit of petering out just when you needed them. At worst they were plain lethal.

Let me give one small, very personal example. For a brief period, I worked as a sub-editor at the local evening newspaper, *The Cambridge Evening News*. While it proudly proclaims itself to be "at the heart of the community", the paper is actually a victim of what Mrs Thatcher called "the great car economy"; produced in a soulless compound next to a concrete factory on an industrial estate some six miles from the city centre. I decided to make the best of a bad thing: I discovered a well signposted cycle path and made a vow that I would keep fit by biking to work each day. This I did – summer and winter – only to find that some civic genius had at one point carefully laid the bike path, with no traffic lights or other warning signs of any description, slap bang across a slip road to the A14. It is at a point where, having negotiated a particularly trying, traffic-choked roundabout, frustrated drivers at last glimpse a clear run and 'go for it', foot down.

It was here one day that I witnessed an admittedly minor and non fatal example of that modern phenomenon 'road rage'. Over the bike path, in front of the oncoming, accelerating cars, rode a brave, bony, pale-faced young-man-in-a-hurry on a racing bike. I watched in amazement as he brandished his fist at a Ford Sierra, one of the cars bearing down on him – causing the surprised driver to brake. The man behind the wheel, red-faced, with close-cropped hair and a tattoo on his neck, gave a blast on his horn. He screamed to a halt, wound down his window and bellowed after the cyclist, "What the f— do you f—ing think you're f—ing doing, you f—ing c—?" The cyclist looked over his shoulder and cried back in firm, stentorian tones, "You should drive more carefully!" Then – wisely – he pedalled on. Thus primed, the Sierra driver set off to join the fuming fray on the A14, dubbed by the *News* 'The Road to Hell' (which I always thought might be just a little unfair on Felixstowe).

I went on my way, chastened and depressed, reflecting that both participants were victims not only of class-ridden backgrounds but also of civic 'muddling through'. However, if you can't beat 'em, you join 'em: when I got home I had a good moan to the missus then went up the road for a pint.

Not long afterwards, I awakened one sunny Saturday to the noise of a helicopter chattering overhead. The sound always reminds me of the Vietnam War, the word 'helicopter' mating most naturally with 'gunship' in my idiolect. All morning as I enjoyed my day off, with the chopper circling overhead, I felt a weird sense of foreboding. The noise of its engines permeated my daily round, triggering semi-conscious reminders of war. I had a feeling that something out of the ordinary was about to happen.

It did.

At about 3pm a ragged procession of people appeared, walking down the middle of Mill Road, blocking the traffic, some of them beating drums. They wore brightly coloured, deliberately torn clothes: faded, slashed denims and ex-Army combats. Many had dreadlocks, others face paint. Incongrously, some trundled old, worn armchairs before them. They were pursued by a small detachment of worried-looking policemen (and women) chattering into walkie-talkies. The helicopter was now directly overhead and lower. When the procession arrived at the top of our street, in front of the aforementioned pub, it halted and several of its members sat down in the road, the wise ones (as it turned out) in armchairs. Others set up a large tripod, blocking the junction. A youngster shinned up it and, perched at its apex, peered into the middle distance like the watch in the crow's nest on an old sailing ship. I asked my next door neighbour what on earth was happening and he said it must be Reclaim the Streets.

"What the devil's that?" I asked.

"I don't really know – some kind of anti traffic demonstration, according to the radio. Didn't you hear the police helicopter this morning?"

Meanwhile more and more people had gathered at the top of the road, a sound system had been set up, the lager was flowing and on came the dancing girls – albeit in Doc Martens, shapeless multi-coloured shifts and with metal studs piercing their lips. Children began chalking on the pavement, youths climbed lampposts, banners were unfurled and wondrous slogans were painted on the railway bridge. One read, 'VEGANS AGAINST MEAT'.

By evening the crowd had grown to several hundred. For all the anarchy, some were there to make a serious point by halting the traffic. This had been achieved the length of Mill Road, from the railway bridge to the Coleridge Road traffic lights – a considerable feat. There was a semblance of organisation. Low-key orders were given, food was distributed, with soft drinks for the children. A couple went around picking up litter and stuffing it in black plastic sacks they had brought with them.

As evening drew nigh, I heard one dreadlocked demonstrator remark (a bit like you or I might say, "Looks a bit like rain"), "Jesus, the f—ing filth's piling up." I thought this odd in view of all the black plastic sacks neatly stacked on the pavement. Then I saw the squadrons of police, tumbling out of vans in full riot gear, some leading snarling Alsatians, and I experienced flashbacks to the Solidarity riots in Communist Poland that I had covered a decade before. Tension mounted. The man in dreadlocks looked up the road and muttered grimly, "Aye, aye, the meat wagon's arrived". It stood under the street light on the railway bridge, large and sinister like something out of a sci-fi movie. But the party continued until a megaphoned voice (in calculatedly reasonable tones that brought back blissful boyhood memories of *Dixon of Dock Green*) called for the demonstrators to dismantle their sound system and go home. It was answered with a cry of "F— off!" and a light shower of empty lager cans. The forces of law and order then moved in. As one tartan-clad, long-haired demonstrator was hauled off struggling towards the 'meat wagon', a woman screamed at the three policemen dragging him, "You're the sad-o's, not him! You're all just so f—ing sad."

But it was all over bar such shouting and the demonstrators knew it. Soon the sound system was packed away, the road cleared and the traffic began flowing again.

I tried to shrug the whole thing off, the way you do, but there was something about the demonstration that disturbed me and my mental stereotype of Britain and the British. These people were not just whingeing about the car, like me, I thought – they were actually **doing** something, muddleheaded and anarchic though that something might be. In the weeks to come, I thought about the demonstration a great deal and for the first time began asking myself some serious questions about the car, the world in general and where it was going. I began looking into what had happened in England while I had been away and I tried to picture how things might develop for good or ill in the future.

FOREWORD
THE DAY AFTER TOMORROW

FUTURE SCENARIO 1:

In a year sometime in the third millennium, on a Sunday in the summer, a family in a town somewhere went for a ride in their car. As they drove, they listened to the news on the radio. The main item concerned yet another serious accident at a nuclear power plant in one of the Russian republics, with scientists saying fall-out would be unlikely to spread to the West. In a follow-up commentary, experts denied that fall-out from several similar though less serious accidents – in Britain, France, Japan and the United States – had been responsible for a dramatic rise in the worldwide incidence of various cancers. There was news too of the thousands of people drowned or forced to move from their homes as a result of flooding caused by global warming and the steady melting of the polar ice caps. In China and South East Asia, more people had been killed in mudslides caused by deforestation. Huge fires raged in the little that remained of the Amazon rain forest, and news was coming in of another huge spill off the new oil fields in Antarctica.

The family listened with foreboding. All of them – father, mother, son and daughter – considered themselves good conservationists. At the bottom of their garden was a large green compost bin where they diligently placed their vegetable peelings. They took their bottles and old newspapers to the community recycling point. They bought their shampoos and cosmetics at The Body Shop, refilling the plastic bottles as they ran out, gaining points on a special card which they traded in for free shampoos and shower gels. Wearing masks to protect them from the pollution, reinforced plastic helmets, sashes of luminous plastic and flashing red lights, the children cycled to school each day. Here they learned how all life depended on delicate, inter-related eco-systems. The little boy read thrilling stories, in books made from recycled paper, about game reserves in Africa and India where lions and tigers had been saved from extinction. The little girl and her friends joined schemes to 'adopt' dolphins and whales. In the evenings there was nothing the family liked more than to watch nature programmes on television.

Conscious that it was a cause of pollution, they generally used their car only for long journeys such as the one they were taking now – to make contact with Nature; to go walking in a national park. Before setting out, they had rubbed barrier cream into their faces and other exposed parts of their bodies to protect them from over exposure to ultra violet rays caused by the depletion of the ozone layer. Until a couple of years ago they might have travelled to the coast to swim in the sea, but nowadays it was nearly always unsafe.

Eventually they left the suburban sprawl of their town behind and joined the motorway. Because it was summer, the garbage thrown from cars – beer cans, cigarette packets, fast food wrappings and the like – was hidden by vegetation, by the laurel, viburnum and alder, great ferns and wildflowers. There were even a few trees left, the little boy noted excitedly. The sun shone down, although it was made hazy by fumes from the densely packed motorway. They joined the other family vehicles and travelled, as they were licenced to do, in the middle lane – passing huge trucks in the slow lane carrying food and goods from one part of the world to another, and being passed in their turn by sleek, high-powered cars with more expensive licences in the fast lane. Many of these were driven by harrassed-looking businessmen, hurrying to keep appointments.

They had not travelled far when a strange thing happened. All the cars and lorries came to a halt and silence fell over the motorway as drivers killed their engines. The phenomenon was called gridlock and was an increasingly common occurrence in this day and age.

But then something unusual happened. In the eerie stillness that prevailed, down the banks of the motorway, streamed a motley crowd of people.

"It's the eco-warriors," shouted the little boy excitedly. "We learn about them in school. There's going to be a demonstration."

His father groaned and slumped despondently over the steering wheel. He had read about such demonstrations in his daily Internet newspaper and knew that they could now be held up here for hours.

More and more people flooded onto the carriageway. They were dressed in ragged, but bright clothes, many with their hair dyed pink or green, and some with old-style, turn-of-the-century dreadlocks. Some carried banners reading 'STOP THE CAR, SAVE THE PLANET', others beat drums and played musical instruments. A group set up a trestle table on the central reservation, took food and drink from hampers and started having a picnic. One man wearing face paint and a clown's costume weaved between the stationary cars and trucks shouting "Climb out of your tin cans and dance!" Other demonstrators began beating a wild tattoo on the roofs of the immobile cars with their bare hands.

Then one group of eco-warriors wearing ex-Army combats, and with their faces obscured by balaclava helmets, began swinging crowbars at the cars in the 'fast' lane, denting bonnets and smashing headlights. In an exaggeratedly theatrical gesture, the people at the picnic table raised glasses of wine to salute them.

A driver in a car that had yet to be attacked picked up his mobile phone and dialled the emergency number. Two of the people with crowbars spotted him and began attacking his car. They wrenched off the door on the driver's side and dragged the man out. They stamped his phone to smithereens and began beating him. A truck driver climbed from his cab swinging a large wrench, obviously intending to go to the aid of the man under attack. He felled two of the eco-warriors but they blew whistles as they went down and soon more of their number arrived at the spot, surrounded the lorry driver, tore the wrench from his hands and beat him to the ground with it.

Our family of good middle-class conservationists watched through the windows of their car, the mother comforting the girl who by this time was whimpering in fear.

"What can we do, Daddy?" asked the boy.

"Nothing," muttered his father grimly. "Just sit tight and wait for the police to get here."

As he spoke there came the sound of helicopters overhead and an angry roar went up from the demonstrators. The men in balaclavas began rocking one of the cars in the fast lane, then overturned it. Petrol spilled from its split fuel tank. The eco-warriors backed off, then lit a torch made of rags. They hurled it at the car which exploded in a ball of fire.

The chatter of the helicopters grew louder and the next minute police in full riot gear came running between the cars, swinging their batons at the demonstrators.

Our family looked on in horror. Then the little girl screamed as one eco-warrior suddenly jumped onto the bonnet of their car, drew back his crowbar and swung it at the windscreen.

Fade to present day reality.

That family does not exist – yet. But there are already plenty like them – well meaning people blind to the shabbiness of their surroundings, who feed only on the glitzy illusions served up to them by television, magazines, newspapers, and the fantasy books they read. They are ordinary people, like you and me, caught in a situation beyond their control; innocent victims of the way the world is seemingly inexorably heading, too busy trying to earn a living to be able to do much about it. There have yet to be anti-car demonstrations quite as violent as the one just described. Yet the seeds for such a confrontation are already sown.

"A grim spectre has crept upon us almost unnoticed, and this imagined tragedy may easily become a stark reality we all shall know."[1] That sentence was written in 1962 by the American biologist Rachel Carson in the opening chapter of her book *Silent Spring*. This concerned the pesticides that were being used on crops and the terrible toll they were taking on the world's wildlife. The 'silent spring' was one in which there would be no birds left to sing. Rachel Carson's book was a landmark to which the roots of today's burgeoning environmental movement may be traced, the outer fringes of which are already occupied by eco-warriors; curious beings in combats and Doc Martens who seem to arrive from nowhere to protest against road building, traffic and despoilation of the Earth in general. They stand outside so called polite society – one dominated, choked and poisoned by cars – proudly seeing themselves as shock troops in a war to stop the world plunging, headless and heedless, into ecological doom.

How fast that world has changed since 1962 can be measured by the fact that when *Silent Spring* was published in Britain it contained a foreword which cited these words:

"We are poisoning the air over our cities; we are poisoning the rivers and the seas; we are poisoning the soil itself. Some of this may be inevitable. But if we don't get together in a real and mighty effort to stop these attacks upon Mother Earth, wherever possible, we may find ourselves one day – one day soon, maybe – in a world that will be only a desert full of plastic, concrete and electronic robots. In that world there will be no more 'nature'; in that world man and a few domestic animals will be the only living creatures. And yet, man cannot live without some measure of contact with nature. It is essential to his happiness."

The jacket of the book contained another quote: "I strongly recommend Rachel Carson's *Silent Spring* if you want to see what is going on."

And whose were these voices crying in the industrial wilderness? The first citation, strong words even with those curious phrases in which the speaker seems to want to hedge his bets – "Some of this may be inevitable ... one day soon, maybe" – was from a speech by Prince Bernhard of the Netherlands, spoken at a Wild Life Fund dinner in London. The second was from HRH The Duke of Edinburgh.

The first chapter of Ms Carson's book was titled 'A Fable for Tomorrow', a fictional look at a future in which birds were extinct. I have borrowed her idea for my Future Scenarios. Ms Carson's last chapter was titled 'The Other Road'.

In it she wrote: "We stand now where two roads diverge. But unlike the roads in Robert Frost's familiar poem, they are not equally fair. The road we have long been travelling is deceptively easy, a smooth superhighway on which we progress with great speed, but at its end lies disaster. The other fork of the road – the one 'less travelled by' – offers our last, our only chance to reach a destination that assures the preservation of our Earth."[2]

David Brower, 'the Archdruid', who in the late 1960s founded

Friends of the Earth, would update the Biblical interpretation of creation for a talk (or rant) he often gave which he called The Sermon. Brower took a scale of 666 million years to each one of the six days of the Bible's version. The earth's initial creation, according to him, took "all day Monday and until Tuesday noon." This was when life began. It then developed over the next four days. "At 4pm Saturday, the big reptiles came in. Five hours later, when the redwoods appeared, there were no more big reptiles. At three minutes before midnight, man appeared. At one-fourth of a second before midnight, Christ arrived. At one-fortieth of a second before midnight, the Industrial Revolution began. We are surrounded by people who think that what we have been doing for that one-fortieth of a second can go on indefinitely. They are considered normal but they are stark, raving mad."[3] Sadly, nothing has changed. Such men still dictate the course the world will take from the boardrooms of the multi-national companies, with the politicians we elect following blindly.

Nearly four decades after *Silent Spring*, humanity is still on the wrong road. All that has happened is that our perverted, polluting societies have taken on board the ecologists who followed up on Ms Carson's work and the protest organisations that came with them, such as Friends of the Earth and Greenpeace. We have allotted them a place in the scheme of things, albeit to one side of the main banquet, where men in grey suits cut the cake that is our world. Our statesmen have learned how to mouth 'green' soundbites while actually doing nothing. The disaffected, radical young have been politically marginalised.

But in a world where seemingly everything can be packaged and sold as a product, there remains a void. Despite all the books, newspapers, glossy magazines and television programmes with their comforting messages of 'business as usual', there is an ever-present anxiety that will not go away. It is in this void, without those in power being aware of it, that the battlelines are being drawn. It is a fact that we are heedlessly still travelling the wrong road, seemingly unable to get off the out-of-control juggernaut called Progress; one that may in the not too distant future call forth onto a gridlocked motorway those eco-warriors with their crowbars and violent, frustrated rage against the car.

YESTERDAY

Yesterday, all my troubles seemed so far away
    - John Lennon and Paul McCartney (Northern Songs)

1

FROM THE GARDEN OF EDEN TO 'AN ENGINE DILATED BY THE COMBUSTION OF GAS'

The idea that once upon a time everything was fine with the world is enshrined in the myths of humanity. Adam and Eve had everything they needed in the Garden of Eden, then they ate from the Tree of Knowledge and the rest, quite literally, is history. The concept of a fall from an initial state of grace runs deep. But the grim reality is that even collective memories are fallible. We still had troubles yesterday, it is just that today seems so much worse that we tuck ourselves up in bed, close our eyes and tell ourselves "Once upon a time…"

The fact of the matter is that the problem of the world's clogged highways and the fumes we choke upon today began in the clean, unpolluted air of yesterday – in the mists of pre-history, with the discovery by some bright spark that tree trunks laid beneath heavy loads make them easier to move. It took a few thousand years, but the next logical step was to cut a section from the trunk, and to fit an axle. Man called it the wheel. Life has never been the same since.

The wheel led inexorably to roads. The Chinese started making them around 4000 BC. No records exist of the vehicles that rolled along these primitive highways but experts say they would most likely have been pulled by men. It took a millennium before some anonymous genius thought of getting an animal to do the job. The first wheeled carts to be recorded by posterity appeared in Sumer and were dragged by asses. Horses would be a later technological advance. The Chinese went down another path and began fitting their carts with sails. It was an interesting, environmentally friendly development that proved a dead end – quite literally so, I imagine, for some of its practitioners on gusty days. By 2500 BC, the Sumerians had forged on to create two different types of war chariot: a heavy 'family' model with four wheels and a light, fast two-wheeled 'sports job' with a single axle.

By now the wheel was really rolling. The Babylonian descendants of Saddam Hussein in 2170 BC built a 2950 feet long tunnel for both riders and wheeled vehicles under the Euphrates. By 600 BC, King Assurbanipal of Assyria was driving a hunting chariot fitted with lightweight wheels, while a mere century further down the line the Persians could boast of their extensive road network, dominated by the amazing 1865 mile Royal Way between Susa and Smyrna.[1] China had a fully developed road system by the end of the Shang dynasty in 11 BC.[2]

The ancient Greeks constructed extremely elegant chariots, often artistically decorated, which they also raced. The Iliad tells how Achilles held a contest outside Troy in honour of Patrocles, his fallen comrade. But Greece was a mountainous land, and overland transport in general was difficult. Roads were often little more than tracks, and travel was primarily by water. "We live around a sea like frogs around a pond," said Socrates, bluntly summing up reliance on seaborne trade and transport.[3] Strange then that the Greeks invented the world's first car – of sorts: records found in the remains of an Athenian temple dating from 1000 BC describe a conveyance that could be powered by its occupants using a system of levers attached to the wheels.

Real traffic difficulties, such as we know them, only started with the Romans. Unlike the Greeks, they laid a heavy emphasis on roads: long, straight ones, precursors of today's motorways. They even constructed a road tunnel over half a mile long connecting Naples and Pozzuoli.[4]

The word 'congestion' derives from the Latin *congestionem*[5], and ancient Rome had plenty of it as this eye-witness account bears testimony: "In hot haste rushes a contractor with mules and porters; a huge crane now hoists a stone and now a beam; mournful funerals jostle massive wagons; this way runs a mad dog: that way rushes a mud-bespattered sow."[6] (While we are at it, the following description of high rise *insulae*, or cheap tenement flats, may ring a bell for many of today's young eco-warriors: "These buildings were in fact temporary refuges rather than real homes and their inhabitants were people passing through: solitary freedmen; young people who had come to the city to launch their career; people on the margins of society."[7] Crash pads, by any other name.)

The Romans had nearly 30 different types of wheeled conveyance, and the world's first real traffic jams resulted from the huge influx of people into the city for the Roman Games each summer.[8] The first person to 'reclaim the streets' – around 45 BC – was Julius Caesar. Shortly before his assassination, the great dictator instituted a law banning from Rome, between sunrise and sunset, carts laden with goods – except those being used to carry building materials. Caesar's motives had nothing to do with improving the environment for his fellow citizens however. He was planning a massive ego-boosting building programme – one that included many road improvements – and wanted his own, unbanned contractors' carts to get through. The ban stayed in place after his death, and Claudius later extended it to other Italian municipalities.[9]

The Romans got a great kick out of speed. Personal chariots, which also escaped Caesar's ban, grew ever lighter and more streamlined, especially those used for racing at the circus – the Formula One of its day. The despotic Nero was particularly fond of chariot racing and once took part in an event at the Olympic Games. A wheel fell off his chariot and he finished last but – the judges obviously not caring to end up as lion-fodder – was still declared the winner.

The number of chariots on the streets of Rome increased alarmingly, causing the Emperor Hadrian to wisely note the contradictory phenomenon we think of as modern: "This luxury of speed destroys its own aim; a pedestrian makes more headway than a hundred conveyances jammed end to end along the twists and turns of the Sacred Way."[10] Substitute 'North Circular' for 'Sacred Way', then get philosophical and ask yourself, "What's new?"

Marcus Aurelius extended the ban on carts to every city in the Roman Empire but injudiciously appointed his son Commodus as his successor. Commodus cared little for wise government but, like Nero, was absolutely crazy about chariot racing. He proved a vastly unpopular emperor and was eventually assassinated. The ill-fated reign of this sad speed freak marked the beginning of the end of the Roman Empire.

Between the 3rd and 18th centuries, the Incas of South America developed a magnificent road system serving an area of some 750,000 square miles. Europe blundered around in the Dark Ages, then stumbled out into the Middle Ages, when poor roads and bands of robbers made movement from place to place exceedingly difficult. The Church established and consolidated its power, and when Roger Bacon in the 13th century forecast that "one day we shall endow chariots with incredible speed without the aid of any animal", rather than being hailed for amazing prescience, he was imprisoned for being in league with the devil.

The first real technological advance since Roman times did not come until the 15th century, with the invention of the pivoted front axle, which greatly improved the manoeuvrability of horse-drawn carriages and carts. Perhaps inspired by this, and bravely nonchalant concerning his proximity to the Vatican, Leonardo Da Vinci (1452-1519) – in addition to painting the Mona Lisa and The Last Supper – found time to design a car. His sketch appears on folio 296 of the *Codex Atlanticus* – though it never got off this antique drawing board. He also suggested segregating pedestrian and wheeled traffic onto different levels in order to beat congestion, which was again rearing its ugly head in Rome.[11]

The number of passenger horse-drawn carriages gradually increased in mainland Europe, but in Britain most travelling was done on foot until the 1600s. The first British passenger coach was built in 1555 for the Duke of Rutland. Sixteen years later Queen Elizabeth I commissioned the first state coach.[12] The historian John Stowe reported: "One William Boonen, a Dutchman brought first the use of coaches hither, and the said Boonen was Queen Elizabeth's coachman, for indeed a coach was a strange monster in those days, and the sight of them put both horse and man into amazement; some said it was a great crab-shell brought out of China, and some imagined it to be one of the Pagan Temples in which the cannibals adored the Devil." The coach's progress was rapid, however, and Stow later reported: "After a while divers great ladies; with a great jealousie of the Queen's displeasure; made their coaches and rid them up and down the country to the great admiration of all the beholders."[13]

Such was progress, that soon congestion in a great many

cities was on a par with that of Caesar's day. By 1520 the civic planners of Paris were warning, "In a few years we will be paralysed."[14] Another decade passed and Sir John Evelyn, in his diary of the 1640s, reported on "the multitude of coaches passing over the bridge, and the large numbers which filled the Tuileries."[15]

In 1649 the Nuremberg clockmaker Johann Hautsch made a self-propelled vehicle which he claimed was driven by a strong clock spring. In reality, several boys were concealed inside to crank it along. It was magnificently decorated and featured a dragon's head at the front that sprayed water over anyone who got in the way. This appealed to the Scandinavian sense of humour: Hautsch sold the original to Swedish Crown Prince Gustav Adolf, then made an even grander model for the King of Denmark.

In London a great deal of transport was waterborne. During the 1660s, Samuel Pepys regularly concluded his diary entries with the words, "And so by water home". The Thames was London's traditional highway, free from the congestion of the streets. When carriages were introduced in London, the Watermen protested in pamphlets that trade was being taken from them: "Coaches and sedans, they deserve both to be throwne into the Thames, and but for stopping the channell (sic), I would they were." John Taylor, a poet who lauded water travel, wrote a leaflet entitled *The World runnes on Wheels* in which he bitterly attacked coaches: "The mischiefs that have been done by them are not to be numbered; as breaking of legs and arms, overthrowing down hills, over bridges, running over children, lame and old people, as Henry the fourth of France, he and his Queen were once like to have been drowned, the coach overthrowing besides a bridge."[16]

Such words of warning had little effect. In 1662 a Mr Cressett added his voice, deploring the increase in the number of stagecoaches on the London-Dover run. They had cut the time taken for the 72 mile journey to three days, and Mr Cressett thought such easy travelling would encourage country gentlemen to come to London for reasons of crass frivolity, such as having their hair cut.[17] By this stage, even Pepys went home by coach, though unwillingly, as shown by this entry in his diary of 1663, "By coach, with a mad coachman, that drove like mad and down byways, through Bucklersbury home – everybody through the streets cursing him, being ready to run over them."

Curiously, the world's first car in the true sense of the word was made far away from such urban pressures. In 1672 Padre Verbiest, a Jesuit priest at the court of the Chinese emperor, who had a passion for mechanical gadgetry "placed an aelopile upon a car and directed the steam generator within it upon a wheel, on which four wheels were attached. The motion thus produced was communicated by gearing to the wheel of the car. The machine continued to move with great velocity as long as the steam lasted, and by means of a helm could be turned in various directions." The description is that of Abbé Hué, writing in *Astronomica Europaea*. Verbiest's actual vehicle is lost to posterity.[18]

Back in Europe, travelling long distances by horse and carriage in anything but perfect summer weather could be horrendous. When Holy Roman Emperor Charles VI visited England in 1703, a 50 mile journey from London to Petworth in Sussex took three days and his carriage overturned a dozen times,[19] while in 1756 the Mile End Road in the East End of London, "resembled a stagnant lake of deep mud" and it was "hard work for four horses pulling a light chaise to go faster than at foot pace."[20] If you think that sounds bad, consider the following description by Arthur Young of the road between Preston and Wigan: "I know not in the whole range of language terms sufficiently expressive to describe this infernal road. Let me seriously caution all travellers... to avoid it as they would the devil." Nowadays you hear people saying much the same about the M25. Daniel Defoe talks of this highway's progenitors in his *A tour through the whole island of Great Britain*, written in 1724, making the point that roads around London had been improved so much that people were starting to move out so they could live in the country and work in town – the dawn of commuting.

France had much better roads than most other European countries – a network of 25,000 paved miles – thanks to the establishment in Paris in 1747 of the Ecole Nationale des Ponts et Chaussées, for the training of engineers.[21] Also in Paris, Captain Nicolas Cugnot began work on a steam driven gun carriage weighing five tons. It is the oldest steam driven vehicle that survives to this day, preserved in the Conservatoire des Arts et Métiers in the French capital. Cugnot demonstrated it to the Duc de Choiseul in 1769. It trundled about for 12 minutes at a speed of six miles per hour, but was so difficult to steer that it ran out of control and demolished a wall.

Most long-distance travel in England was on foot and still in appalling conditions. The upkeep of roads had previously been the responsibility of the parishes through which they ran, and was unwillingly undertaken. As a result the turnpike system of making travellers pay tolls to use roads was introduced and slowly brought some improvement. The only trouble was that the system was frequently abused by the trusts running the turnpikes, and it became a source of great public resentment. There were riots in Somerset, Gloucester and Hereford in the late 1720s, and incidents of toll gates being destroyed and collectors assaulted over the next two decades. This unrest culminated in a fairly serious riot in Leeds in 1753.[22]

But if you coughed up your toll unprotestingly and used the turnpike, pollution on it would be quite appalling. The offenders, I regret to say, were animals. Around the close of the 18th century 100,000 Highland cattle a year were being driven south to London. From 1776-1785, 992,040 beef cattle and 6,859,990 sheep were driven to Smithfield Market.[23] Such movements, along with those of pigs and other livestock, turned unpaved roads into insanitary quagmires and it was generally accepted until the late 18th century that wheeled traffic could not travel on them for at least four or five months of the year. When it did, breakdowns frequently occurred, as this entry in the Post Office archives for November 21 1796 testifies: "The down coach, No. 35, was left at Rochester last night with the off hind wheel broke ... Exeter [mail coach had to be] changed at Salisbury after wheel broke, Shrewbury ditto... Oxford ditto..."[24]

Biological pollution levels were high on all roads, both in the country and in town. A report in the *Architectural Review* cites the following eye witness report from the turn of the century: "The whole of London's crowded wheeled traffic – which in parts of the city was dense beyond movement – was dependent on the horse. The characteristic aroma was that of stables... whose middens kept the chandeliers in middle-class reception rooms ... encrusted with dead flies, and in the late summer veiled with living clouds of them. A more assertive mark of ze 'orse was the mud that… flooded the street with churnings of pea soup that … covered the road surface with axle grease or bran-laden dust. The swift-moving hansom or gig would fling sheets of such soup – where not intercepted by trousers or skirts – completely across the pavement, so that the frontages of the Strand had an eighteen inch plinth of mud parge thus imposed upon it. And after the mud the noise, which, again endowed by the horse, surged like a mighty heart-beat in the central districts of London's life. It was a thing beyond all imaginings… It was not any such paltry thing as noise. It was an immensity of sound…"[25]

The beginnings of the steam age and the Industrial Revolution at the close of the 18th century only made things worse. Thomas Carlyle described 19th century London as the "noisiest Babylon that ever raged and fumed on the face of the earth."

Early attempts to adapt steam to the roads failed, albeit valiantly. In 1801 Richard Trevithick, a Cornish mining engineer, successfully climbed Cambourne Beacon in his 'dragon', a steam carriage he made in his blacksmith's works. One of a party of workmen who travelled with him described the event thus: "When we see'd that Captain Dick was a'going to turn on steam, we jumped on as many as could, maybe seven or eight of us. T'was a stiffish hill, but she went up like a bird." In the best tradition of inventors, Captain Dick was a trifle absent-minded and left the fire burning when garaging his vehicle in the stables of a local hotel. The resulting inferno destroyed every trace of the vehicle – and with it the hotel.[26] Despite this and other mishaps, the quest for a steam-driven car continued.

The Industrial Revolution had made new forms of transport imperative. Manufacturers had hitherto depended upon canals and rivers to shift the goods they were producing, but this was inefficient. The Industrial Revolution changed the way men thought of travel and living. As Professor John Whitelegg, head of the Lancaster-based transport and environment consultancy Ecologica, puts it, "The industrial revolution in Europe ushered in a major space-time restructuring so that leaving home and travelling to work became part of everyday life and mechanical, measured time became part of everyday consciousness."[27]

Heeding this imperative, an Englishman called Samuel Brown

invented a car with a slow-burning internal combustion engine, which in 1826 he drove up Shooters Hill in London. It was not considered practical and elsewhere the emphasis was entirely on steam.[28] The railways arrived and around the same time, Goldsworthy Gurney's 'new steam coach' began to cruise at a sedate five miles per hour around Regent's Park, attracting this anonymous tribute in verse:

> *Instead of journeys, people now*
> *May travel on a Gurney*
> *With steam to do the horse's work*
> *By Pow'r of Attorney.*

By 1834, Walter Hancock had revolutionised wheel design with his 'wedge' model, the forerunner of that used on the modern car. When it came to road travel, the limitations of the steam engine soon became obvious, and the race was now seriously set to find a viable alternative. The world's first internal combustion engine, powered by the explosion of gas, was most likely made in 1857 at a foundry in Florence by Eugenio Barsanti and Felice Matteuci. However, they delayed in taking out a patent, allowing Etienne Lenoir, a more ruthlessly dynamic Parisian, to pass into history on January 24 1860 as the inventor of "an engine dilated by the combustion of gas." The vehicle Lenoir made to accommodate his engine was heavy and slow, and its maximum speed a mere four miles per hour. Its inventor drove it for a while through the Bois de Vincennes between his home and his workshop but then lost interest. His car was later destroyed in the Franco-Prussian War.

Siegfried Marcus, an Austrian, invented the first petrol-engine car, unveiled at the 1873 Vienna Exhibition, whilst in 1886 Hans Johansen, a Dane, built a vehicle that still runs to this day – albeit at a speed of only six miles per hour. The motoring age only truly began, however, in 1888 when Carl Benz of Mannheim began marketing a *patent motorwagen*, a two-seater tricycle powered by a petrol driven engine. Another German engineer, Gottlieb Daimler, followed up with a true horseless carriage – he took one hitherto pulled by a nag, reinforced its frame and fitted it with a motor. This prototype is preserved in the Deutsches Museum in Munich. The vehicle he made, a four-wheeled two-seater with a tubular steel frame, caused a sensation at the World Fair held in Paris in 1889.

It was the French who first followed up German pioneer work on the car; Armand Peugeot, Count Albert de Dion, René Panhard and Emile Levassor all contributing to its development. Britain, still in those days a green, pleasant and vastly conservative land, led world opposition to the car with the Locomotive Act of 1865. This stipulated that any machine-powered vehicle must be accompanied by at least three drivers, could drive at a maximum speed of only four miles per hour in open country, two miles per hour in town, and had to be preceded (until 1878) by a man on foot, preferably holding a red flag.

This had the effect of greatly stimulating production of the newly invented bicycle as a faster alternative. Bicyclists were at first abominated as "ironmongery riders" and "cads on castors" and accused of using the highway while contributing nothing for its upkeep. It was not until 1888, by which time JB Dunlop's pneumatic tyres had made cycling far more comfortable and popular, that the law declared the bike to be a carriage legally entitled to use the roads. The few cars on the roads were all imported from the Continent, and – having by this time well and truly fallen from any mythical state of grace Britain might once have occupied – it was there that the first round of 'car wars' was about to be fought.

2
POST-CHAISES
AND PINK CADILLACS

Eco-warriors, crusties, campaigners for social justice and the plain down-trodden (and often envious), find common ground in their derision of gas guzzling cars as symbols of wealth and status. The rise of the *nouveau riche* has seen an increase in the display of wealth in this way. Elvis had his collection of pink Cadillacs, John Lennon his psychedelic Rolls-Royce. But there were pockets of resistance. Let us make a detour to Nashville, where in the 1970s Dick Feller wrote *Lord Mr Ford*, a very funny anti-car song, later recorded by guitar-picker Jerry Reed:

> *Now Lord, Mr Ford, I just wish that you could see*
> *What your simple horseless carriage has become*
> *Well, it seems your contribution to man*
> *To say the least has got a little out of hand*
> *Well, Lord, Mr Ford what have you done?*

One of the verses concludes:

> *But the thing that amazes me I guess,*
> *Is the way we measure a man's success*
> *By the kinda automobile he can afford to drive*[1]

Well, as someone else once said long before Mr Reed picked up his guitar, *Plus ça change, plus c'est le même chose.*[2] The Sumerians, Romans and Greeks all had their fancy chariots and other vehicles designed to emphasise their importance. And in the 18th century, the horse-drawn carriage was every bit the status symbol the car can be today. In her novels, Jane Austen

27

often refers to carriages to establish the position of her characters in society: "Well, my dear," said Mrs Jennings, "and how did you travel?" "Not in the stage, I assure you," replied Miss Steele, with quick exultation; "we came post all the way, and had a very smart beau to attend us. Dr Davies was coming to town, and so we thought we'd join him in a post-chaise; and he behaved very genteelly, and paid ten or twelve shillings more than we did."[3]

So too by the latter part of the century, the carriage had become for the vast majority of the population of France a highly visible symbol of oppression. At that time, France had a total population of around 23 million people, of whom a mere 400,000 were members of the nobility. The carriages of this privileged minority would rattle – curtains firmly drawn on plush, perfumed interiors – past scenes of the most appalling poverty imaginable. One man who did look out was Arthur Young, an English landowner who travelled extensively in France at the time. He wrote of countrywomen and ploughmen without shoes or stockings and of children "terribly ragged, if possible worse clad than if with no cloaths (sic) at all".[4] The novelist Tobias Smollett said the peasants looked more like "ravenous scarecrows" than human beings. In a Paris seething with social and political unrest, the carriages of the ruling class raced through the streets for fear of the mob. An eye witness account spoke of the "threatening wheels of the overbearing rich (who) drive as rapidly as ever over streets stained with the blood of their victims".[5]

It was such pent-up anger that spilled over in the Revolution of 1789; the streets of the capital became stained with the blood of royalty, the aristocracy and finally that of the revolutionaries themselves, as they divided into factions and fought each other. This terrible event was to shape the ideology and politics of the 19th century as much as the British Industrial Revolution would shape its economy.[6] Attitudes formed in these times would play their part in the evolution of the car and the struggle against it.

The influence of the French Revolution was felt far and wide at the time. Ordinary working men and women began to realise that by joining together they could do something about their miserable lot in life. In Nottingham in 1811, the Luddites smashed textile machinery which they feared would put them out of work, and the first major anti-road demonstration followed, in the winter of 1842-43. It was bizarrely coupled with an outbreak of mass cross-dressing. Anger at the inefficient and dishonest extraction of tolls on turnpike roads in South Wales turned to rioting with toll houses burned down and gates demolished. The rioters – most of them chapel goers – were inspired by Genesis 24:60: "And they blessed Rebecca, and said to her, "Our sister, be the mother of thousands of ten thousands; and may your descendants possess the gate of those who hate them!" Thus, the unlikely spectacle of a concerted attack on the toll gates by burly Welsh peasant farmers, dressed as women and calling themselves 'Rebecca and her Children'. Although in law they faced the death penalty for such an insurrection, the rioters were treated leniently – many were simply bound over to keep the peace. The Home Secretary, Sir James Graham, pushed through reforms that eroded the power of the turnpike trusts and led to greatly improved road maintenance.

The first car to arrive in Britain was, in all probability, an 1888 Roger Benz three-wheeler, like the model exhibited at the Paris World Fair of 1889. It is now in the Science Museum in Kensington, London. Museum records show only that it was purchased from a Mrs EB Bath of King's Lynn, Norfolk in 1913 for just £5. Quite a bargain, all things considered.

Back on the Continent, barely a century had passed since the Revolution when a new privileged class began to invade the roads of France – this time in horseless carriages. The French reacted true to type: there were violent protests.

The thousands of cars on the streets of Paris, driven by a rich minority, were regarded with suspicion, even hatred, by ordinary citizens. In 1897 after he had been knocked down in the Bois de Boulogne by a car "going at the speed of an express train", Hugues le Roux wrote a furious letter to the Prefect of Police denouncing motorists as "mad dogs". Le Roux said that in future when he went walking he would carry a loaded revolver and shoot anyone he encountered driving a car. Appalled, *La Locomotion Automobile*, an early French motoring magazine, hit back with a declaration that if Le Roux made good his threat, motorists would defend themselves with machine guns.[7]

It is doubtful the car that hit le Roux really was going that fast: a year after the incident, the world speed record stood at a little below 40mph.[8] However, the de Dion car firm seemed only too happy to inflame a delicate situation still further. Their advertising posters emphasised the aristocratic insouciance of de Dion drivers, picturing them sitting aloof with their women passengers as they ran over pigs and geese. Total world production of motor vehicles in 1903 was 61,927, of which 30,204 were made in France.[9] Statistics for deaths of pigs and geese are not recorded.

When a motorist careened out of control into a wedding procession in Boulogne in 1903 there were riots, while in Fontainebleu when another driver ran over a pedestrian, an angry mob burned his car.[10]

In more conservative England, the car was at this time generally regarded as a Continental flash in the pan that would most likely come to nothing. Consequently there were very few of them to be seen. In 1903 there were 17,000 motor vehicles registered in Britain, of these 8,000 were cars (0.2 per 1,000 population), 4,000 were goods vehicles and 5,000 public transport vehicles.[11] The Manchester artist LS Lowry would tell friends how, before the turn of the century, his then upwardly mobile parents moved to Victoria Park, a private estate where "Gothic palaces jostle each other and gardeners dust the soot from the leaves of the trees". The estate had toll gates manned by uniformed keepers, and horse drawn trams were banned. The car was eventually admitted but only in the belief that "only two or three of the inhabitants of the district would ever use them". Youthful perspectives are experienced deeply. Shelly Rohde, Lowry's biographer, says, "Lowry was 21 years old before he left Victoria Park, so this perhaps accounts for the remark with which he astonished a friend in Huddersfield in the late fifties: 'Don't those cars over there look funny – all going along without horses.'"[12]

In Lowry's youth the 'Red Flag Act' imposed severe restrictions on the relatively few cars that were imported. Horses remained the dominant means of getting from A to B. Motorists were obliged to stop and switch off their engines when they encountered a horse driven vehicle, or farm animals being herded.

The case for the car was not helped by some of those promoting it. In 1895 the flashy and flamboyant entrepreneur

Harry Lawson with two equally dodgy colleagues, Martin Rucker and Terrence Hooley (later jailed for fraud), set up the British Motor Syndicate Ltd. This company bought the British rights to Daimler, and then resold them at an inflated price to an associated company. The process was repeated with other foreign cars, greatly adding to the wealth of Messrs Lawson, Rucker and Hooley, but doing little to advance motoring. One of the trio's firms, grandly titled the Great Horseless Carriage Company, produced not one single vehicle and was finally reorganised at great cost to its shareholders as the Motor Manufacturing Company. Unlike Hooley, Lawson – who liked to call himself the "Father of the British Motor Industry" – stayed just the right side of the law. When he did finally begin manufacturing cars, he claimed they were "British throughout", despite the fact that most of their components were imported.

Other cars that were manufactured domestically were copies of foreign models. The Talbot was based on the French Clément, the Crossley on the Mercedes and the Weigel on the Italia. In 1895 when Sir David Salomons held Britain's first Motor Show at his house near Tunbridge Wells, he could muster only six exhibits.

There was one exception to the rule. In the same year, the first wholly British four-wheeled car, the Lanchester, was given a test run though it did not go into production until 1900. Meanwhile, in 1896, the 'Red Flag Act' was replaced by the so-called Emancipation Act, which raised the speed limit to 14mph. The last motorist to be fined for speeding before it was passed was Walter C Bersey, a designer of electric cars and buses. He was summoned on two counts: not having a footman preceeding his car at a distance of 20 yards, and because he did "unlawfully drive a certain locomotive, to wit, a motor car, through a certain town at a greater speed than 2 miles an hour."

The first recorded British accident involving a car happened in 1896. A Mrs Driscolls of London was knocked down on her way to the theatre by a vehicle travelling at four miles an hour. An inquest ruled that the unfortunate woman had been a victim of her own negligence.

People were still highly suspicious, even afraid, of the new invention. The Hon Charles Rolls, soon to make motoring history by going into business with Henry Royce, described a trip he made to his home in Monmouth from Cambridge: "In the country... when the car was moving every other man climbed up a tree or telegraph pole to get out of the way, every woman ran away across the fields, every horse jumped over the wall and every butcher's cart that was left at the side of the road with the tailboard down, bolted off, scattering various parts of animals along the road. I even saw some old ladies jump over the wall of a churchyard. We passed a field with farm labourers working near the edge of the road; the whole company ran away at full speed across the big field!"[13]

Rolls had an almost religious fervour for motoring. On a trip to France one winter, he had to dismantle part of the transmission on the open road between Paris and Le Havre. Shelley Rolls, his sister, waited in the car as he did so. Her story bears witness to the indignities suffered by the early motorists and their consorts: "Some hours later, in order to shelter from the snow, I myself got partly underneath the car. I was just in time to witness the final unbolting of the gearcase. I saw it drop on my brother's chest together with all the black oil the gearbox had contained. He was in a terrible state with the conglomeration of tallow and oil."[14]

The first British car crash in which the driver was killed came in July 1899: Edwin Sewell and his passenger Major Richie died when the rear wheel of their Coventry Daimler collapsed as they climbed Grove Hill, Harrow, and they were thrown out of the car.

Such incidents helped to fuel distrust in the new invention. Queen Victoria described the car as "a very shaky and disagreeable conveyance altogether."[15] Her Majesty's preferred mode of long distance travel was train. Pages, servants, dressers, ladies' maids, ladies-in-waiting, courtiers and railway company directors travelled with her. The royal coaches were elaborately padded and panelled to prevent noise and vibration. Lines were cleared for each journey and drivers of other trains passing had to do so "very quietly" at 10 miles an hour, with no letting off steam or blowing of whistles. Another train travelled 15 minutes ahead of HM to make sure all these conditions were adhered to.

The Queen was not alone in being unamused by "the infernal combustion engine". Many still believed steam a more viable alternative. Again the French led the way. Léon Serpollet's steam cars looked like giant hard-boiled eggs and could easily hold their own with the petrol-fuelled variety. Powered by boilers that were heated by paraffin, causing less pollution than coal or wood, Serpollet's cars were light, quiet and reached speeds of up to 80mph. In 1900, Herbert Austin – after experimenting with copies of French models – began to manufacture cars for his employers the Wolseley Sheep Shearing Company. In the same year, Serpollet produced and sold 200 steam cars and his clients included the Prince of Wales (later Edward VII) and the Shah of Persia.[16]

The petrol driven car was by now a favourite target for cartoonists. Its detractors were gleefully triumphant when a mile race between a horse pulling a sulky and a petrol-driven car (a de Dion-Bouton) ended in a virtual dead-heat.

Much British opposition to the car stemmed from a deep distrust of innovation. This set in as the Industrial Revolution began to change the face of the countryside and gave premonition of still greater upheavals to come. It was also a fact that in a country bedevilled by one of the most entrenched class systems in the world, car owners were looked down upon by the landed gentry as "illiterate and grease-stained boors". The car, initially taxed as a "four wheel carriage", was seen as a diabolical attempt to gain admission by the backdoor to the "carriage-owning classes".[17] Some idea of the degree of prestige accorded to the carriage may be gauged from the fact that many motorists carried riding crops similar to those used by carriage owners as a fashion accessory. Some cars were even fitted with brackets to hold them.[18]

A campaign by such *parvenu* horseless carriage enthusiasts to raise the speed limit was dourly resisted, with *The Times* capturing the mood of the day in a leading article that thundered, "the number of drivers of motor cars who are not gentlemen would seem to be unduly large. There is no turning a cad into a gentleman, but there is such a thing as making even cads fear the law."[19] The early motorist was lampooned in the music halls as "a begoggled monster who spent rare moments of ecstatic motion, scattering hens, dogs, children and old women in terror before his dust cloud and weary hours stranded by the roadside struggling with recalcitrant and incomprehensible machinery."[20]

The police, who in Victorian and Edwardian England were generally treated as lackeys by the upper classes, without doubt would sometimes take out their resentments on motorists by falsely accusing them of speeding. But even honest attempts to enforce speed limits met with opposition that did not sit well with the general public. Motorists complained that methods used were unscientific and arbitrary. They had a definite point. The standard police trap involved two constables timing the car over a measured distance, often with ordinary as opposed to stop watches. The Hon Evelyn Ellis, son of Lord Howard de Walden, protested by driving through Windsor at 12-14mph – though he was so well known and his family so influential that the local police took no action.[21]

Fuel was extremely difficult to come by. In many cases drivers would be reliant on bottles purchased at the chemist, or maybe in a grocery store or pub. Headlamps burned acetylene gas, which was similarly difficult to find. The early motorists saw themselves as pioneers. One was Rudyard Kipling, who in 1904, wrote: "I love motoring because I have suffered for its sake... My agonies, shames, delays, rages, chills, parboilings, road-walkings, water-drawings, burns and starvations – at which you laughed – all went to make your car today safe and comfortable... Any fool can invent anything, as any fool can wait to buy the invention when it is thoroughly perfected, but the men to reverence, to admire, to write odes and erect statues to, are those Prometheuses and Ixions (maniacs, you used to call us) who chase the inchoate idea to fixity up and down the King's Highway with their red right shoulders to the wheel... I love because I have suffered... in the cause of Humanity."

Speed exacerbated one of the principal reasons for public animosity towards the car: environmental pollution in the form of the mini-dust storms it created on the unsealed roads of the time. The horse-drawn water cart, brought in to settle dust on roads in the pre-car era, could no longer cope. Motorists themselves suffered greatly from the dust clouds and had to drive in ankle-length coats, masks, scarves and goggles, even in summer. Some drivers fitted a canvas dust screen at the rear of the car. There were various other shields and deflectors aimed at stopping dust clouds from forming. The Automobile Club's Anti-Dust Trials, held in 1908, featured a weird and wonderful collection of ideas to beat the menace. These included mechanically-driven brushes sweeping a path ahead of the car wheels and a giant vacuum cleaner driven from the gear box, which sucked in dust from pipes positioned behind each wheel. The smoother the underbelly of the car, the less dust. The Dutch Spyker car's nether regions were so smooth, it earned the sobriquet 'The Dustless Spyker'. Finally, it was realised that the real solution to the dust problem lay in sealing the roads with tar then adding granite or limestone chips.

The counties, who were responsible for the upkeep of roads, greatly resented the motorists who now began to invade them. Surrey, Sussex, Kent and Middlesex were particularly tough on drivers, most of whom came from London. Magistrates were usually from the minor landowning or retired officer classes. They were particularly fond of horses and were hard on motorists, often accepting evidence that really should have been laughed out of court. One infamously zealous sergeant worked on his own to trap cars he could not even see, relying on timing the speed of an approaching dust cloud, and a Surrey JP would frequently take to the 'front line', pelting passing motorists with clods of garden refuse.[22]

While rarely stooping to the violent lengths favoured by the French, sometimes even generally docile everyday English country folk would take the law into their own hands against incursions into their territory by motorised city dwellers. The racing driver and entrepreneur SF Edge was driving through Crawley one particularly cold winter's day when a local man hurled a rock at him. The rock hit Edge on the head and, enraged, he stopped his car and chased the "yokel", as he later described him, through two snow-filled fields. Edge caught up with his assailant, wrestled him to the ground, and stripped him down to his underpants and shoes. He then drove off with the rest of the man's clothes, leaving them at the next village. It was, Edge noted with some satisfaction, one of the coldest nights of the year.[23]

The speed limit was finally, in 1903, raised to 20mph in an Act of Parliament that also obliged motorists to register their cars and display identification plates. But motorists protested that even this was too low and demanded the lifting of all limits. The bill was resisted in the House of Commons by anti-motoring MPs who described it as "government of the rich, for the rich and by the rich." Some MPs said motoring helmets and goggles were a disguise for people who intended to break the law. One member called for errant motorists to be flogged, another said they should be imprisoned.[24] Car drivers dismissed it all as 'motorphobia' and responded by forming the Automobile Association, which sent out squads of scouts on bicycles to locate police speed traps and warn drivers approaching them. When a patrol did not salute, it meant there was a trap ahead.

By 1909 the trendsetting Rolls-Royce made its debut, securing many upper class converts to the cause of the car and setting new standards of refinement, economy and reliability. The Royal Automobile Club calculated its running costs at fourpence halfpenny a mile. Other less luxurious cars by this time cost as little as twopence a mile.[25]

In America too there was initially considerable opposition to the introduction of cars. A New York alderman unsuccessfully proposed a ban on gasoline within the city limits, while Chicago banned people wearing glasses from driving.

Magistrate Kellogg of Yonkers waged his own personal vendetta against motorists with a 'flying squad' of bicycling speed cops. The magazine *Automobile Topics* wrote: "Encouraged by his petty despotism every village constable in the northern suburb now seems to regard himself as a heaven-sent lawmaker, confident that whatever legal freaks his brain may engender, a ready sponsor will be found on the local bench." Mayor Dennis of Glencoe, Illinois, went one better by stringing steel cables across the main road to stop cars entering his territory. When he was sued and ordered to remove them, he ordered that the road be dug up into artificial bumps – primitive ancestors to today's 'sleeping policemen'.

In the good old 'no nonsense' tradition of the windy city, police on Chicago's North Shore Drive began opening fire on drivers who ignored their speed traps, and the magazine *Motor Age* announced that war had been declared.

Just as they were in Europe, cars were the playthings of the rich. Cornelius Vanderbilt IV would flout the law in his huge red tourer, 'losing' police on the streets of New York. In 1905 the multi-millionaire Pierpont Morgan was declared guilty of a hit and run in which a pedestrian had been injured. He escaped prosecution when his victim withdrew her complaint but the case became something of a *cause célèbre*. Future President Woodrow Wilson commented, "Nothing has spread socialistic feeling in this country more than the use of the automobile. To the countryman they are a picture of arrogance and wealth, with all its independence and carelessness."

While Cadillac concentrated on producing top quality cars in the US ('The Standard of the World'), the first models to reach a popular market were those made by Ransom Eli Olds in Detroit. Henry Ford experimented briefly with steam but concluded, "to be seated on a high-pressure engine which might explode is not a pleasant thought." A good man for the *bon mot*, Henry: he thought history "bunk" and also famously said, "The customer can have the car in any colour he wants – as long as it is black." Eventually he founded his own company manufacturing cars driven by the internal combustion engine and, in the best plagiaristic traditions of capitalism, undercut Olds to become the world's largest car manufacturer. In 1907 his production lines began churning out 'model Ts', popularly known as 'Tin Lizzies', the first really successful mass-produced cars. They stayed in production for 18 years and a grand total of 15,176,888 were made. An enterprising American pastor even converted one into a mobile chapel. In 1913 the Lincoln transamerican highway was opened, linking New York and San Francisco.

Back in Britain cars were still largely the prerogative of the rich. The president of the Local Government Board, which imposed speed limits, summed up the situation: "There is an embittered feeling in the general public against all persons who use motor-cars, which as a dangerous class feeling, is, perhaps, without parallel in modern times."

The Highways Protection League, which had been formed in 1903, castigated the car as a menace on the roads and called for the jailing of drivers who broke the speed limit. Motoring organisations responded by organising a nationwide series of 'stopping trials' to prove that cars could halt in half, and sometimes a quarter, of the distance required by a horse and carriage. In one such test held at the Crystal Palace, a butcher's cart travelling at 12mph took 50 feet to come to a standstill, while a 15 horsepower De Dion going at the same speed stopped in less than 10 feet. A trotting sulky travelling at 20mph took 43 feet; a 90 horsepower Napier just 26 feet. While in another test in Hertford "it was reported that the coachman at the reins of a four-wheel dog-cart was so humiliated by a Lanchester that he broke down and wept."[26]

The King, Edward VII, did a great deal to popularise the car. He had taken his first ride in a petrol-driven car, a 12 horsepower Daimler, in 1899 and enjoyed it so much that he later bought a number of cars and ordered that the Royal Mews at Buckingham Palace be converted to accommodate them. He agreed to be patron of the 1903 Automobile Exhibition, forerunner of today's Motor Show. He had even considered using a petrol-driven coach for his coronation, but stipulated that it should be "without noticeable vibration, noise, smell or vapour", which was too much to ask for in those days. Edward did not approve of breakdowns, seeing them as a personal affront. When they occurred he would say coldly to his chauffeur, "This should not be."[27]

But motoring remained a chancy venture. *The Autocar* recommended the following accessories to be taken on ordinary runs: "accumulator (spare); aprons and rugs, Burners for acetylene lamps; Carbide; complete contact breaker for magneto, with platinum contacts and slip-ring carbon brush; Engine valve and valve spring, etc, complete; Files (round and flat); Gauges for setting magneto contact and sparking plug gaps; Grease and injector; Hammer; Hand vice; Horn; Inner tubes (two, in bags); Insulating tape; Jack; Lamps; Nuts, bolts and washers (various); Oils (paraffin and engine); Oilcans (two) for above; Petrol in spare tin (two gallons); Pliers (large and small); Screwdrivers (large and small); Spanners (box and tubular) to fit all nuts; Spare wheel, complete with inflated tyre; Sparking plugs and washers (four); Split pins; Spring washers; Straps: Twine and cord; Tyre inflator; Tyre levers (fork lever for valve insertion); Tyre repair outfit, with chalk and solution; Tyre valve parts; Voltmeter (if batteries are carried); Washers, metal and copper asbestos; Wire (copper 16g, iron 20g and 30g, and high-tension and low tension insulated wire); Wrenches (large and small)."[28]

Despite such necessities, the car was very definitely here to stay. In the first five years of the 20th century, the number of cars in Britain rose from 1,000 to 8,400 and in the US from 8,000 to 79,000.[29] In Britain the government recognised the car as a money spinner – Lloyd George's budget of 1909 introduced taxation of motor vehicles with the receipts allocated to a Road Fund, and taxed petrol at threepence a gallon. Opposition to the car continued. A poster from this period read: "Men of England. Your birthright is being taken from you by Reckless Motorists. Reckless Motorists drive over and kill your children. Reckless motorists drive over and kill both men and women. Reckless motorists kill your dogs. Reckless motorists kill your chickens. Motorists fill your houses with dust. Motorists spoil your clothes with dust. Motorists, with dust and stink, poison the air we breathe."[30]

By the time Edward VII died in 1910, motorised bicycles, tri-cars and 'cycle cars' began to bring motoring down to working class level. Treasury returns for England and Wales, for 1911-1912, show licence duty paid on 31,260 cabs and omnibuses, and 144,328 other vehicles. There were still pockets of resistance – Sir Osbert Sitwell records a letter written to him by his grandmother in 1913: "I think motors are such dangerous, horrid, odious things, and always feel ill for days after I have been in one."[31] Up until the outbreak of World War One, cars continued to be seen largely as rich men's playthings, costing as much in comparative terms before 1914 as they did in the 1960s.[32] There was relentless advance. By the time war was declared, it was estimated that there were a quarter of a million mechanical vehicles of all types in Britain. Buses were a fact of life and horse-drawn vehicles rarely seen in cities. Crown magazine was able to report, "To the man in the street the motor-car must have remained a pernicious and unwholesome thing for ever, had it not been for the happy advent of the motor-omnibus. You cannot go on very well hating motors when you are constantly taking penny rides in them."[33]

The war was a watershed. As it dragged on, bogged down in mud and human misery, its horrors acted as a spur for change. The Bolsheviks seized power in Russia, and elsewhere in Europe socialism and a relentless drift towards democracy gained pace. With peace finally a fact, very different social conditions prevailed. Yet there was a hiatus before mass production gained ground, a blissful period beloved by those who look back fondly to those yesterdays when all our troubles seemed so far away, before the car began to change the face of the world – when it was itself a thing of elegance and beauty and a great liberator, albeit only for a privileged minority. That period is known as 'The Golden Age of Motoring'.

3
SUNNY DAYS WITH JAMES, DARK DAYS WITH HITLER

Democracy, along with efficiency and speed, has become one of the components of the ideal we think of as Progress. We use it as an excuse to cover a multitude of sins: if something is democratic it must be for the good – the customer is always right. Uncomfortable though it may be to admit it, this is not always the case. When it comes to the car, democracy is largely to blame for the mess we are in today. It is the ideal of 'motoring for everyman' that makes the car simultaneously so seductive a product and yet such a menace. If only we could have frozen events in The Golden Age of Motoring, that period between the wars, things would have been fine. Then, the car posed but a minimal threat to the environment and its benefits, even though enjoyed only by a privileged few, were manifest. Between 1920 and 1930 the annual increase of cars in use stayed fairly constant at 80,000-100,000 a year. This reflected a steady increase in the standard of living but one that was restricted to the middle classes. It was only in the 1930s that the danger signs first began to appear.

Sitting in a traffic jam on a crowded city road, even bowling unimpeded down a modern motorway, it is difficult – if not impossible – to imagine motoring as it must have been in the first decades of the 20th century. Roads were uncluttered, the view from them was genuinely pastoral and outside major cities there was no traffic to speak of. Even in crowded Britain, Cornwall and Scotland were still exotic, far away places for car owners from London. There was champagne and foie gras in the picnic hamper, and the car was such a novelty that even a whiff of Castrol had a certain *je ne sais quoi*. Similarly, in an age in which cars come off production lines and the various makes look very much like one another, it is difficult to remember that once upon a time – not really so very long ago – cars actually had real character and individuality, if you could afford them, which was a big "if". The carriage owning classes had now, by and large, succumbed to the internal combustion engine. But of course, one absolutely had to employ someone in uniform to drive it for you.

Consider this advice on how to deal with a chauffeur in the *Continental Touring Guide for Motorists Abroad*: "Keep a firm hand on him, but treat him well. It is to the employer's profit that he should be kept in good health and temper. Touring engenders sluggishness and too easy-going habits. Let him see before starting that a high standard of work will be expected of him." The right clothing is essential, says the guide, "Otherwise he may get sunstroke in Italy and pneumonia on the Swiss passes. This is awkward for his master."[1] And none too pleasant for the poor chauffeur, of course.

The editor of a motoring magazine received the following inquiry, "Sir – Will you tell me if you consider that a chauffeur is entitled to an annual holiday? To me it seems that here, at any rate, is a trade where such a privilege should not be allowed to become one of the ever-increasing 'rights' of those who serve us. The primary object of a holiday, I take it, is to afford the tired town-worker a short period of rest, and fresh air, and a change of scenery and surroundings, and to such the annual holiday is a just and beneficent institution. I cannot but think, however, that a motor-man comes under another category altogether. My man's life seems to me to be one continual round of enjoyment. Touring all through the summer months supplies him with all the fresh air and change of scenery he may require; during the winter, beyond a month or six weeks on the Riviera the car goes out but little, and he is then able to enjoy whatever rest may be necessary.

"I have to supply my chauffeur with a singularly good and reliable car, and year out year in beyond the ordinary routine work (petrol, oil, grease, water etc.) his duties are limited to mending an occasional puncture, all washing, polishing, etc. being done in the garage and charged in the bill; for this I pay him £3 per week and his expenses when away from London. And yet he asked me this morning when it would be convenient that he should take 'his holiday'.

"Now, sir, I have no wish to appear a hard task-master or to contravene any custom, but do you not think that this is asking too much?"[2]

The story is told of a duchess who, when her regular chauffeur did have the effrontery to take a holiday, hired a replacement from an agency. "What is your name?" she asked the new man.

"James, Your Grace."

"Christian name or surname?"

"Christian name, Your Grace."

"Oh. Well, I would prefer to use your surname. What is it?"

"Darling."

"Drive on, James."[3]

The instruction book for a 1912 Humberette read: "The RAC rating is 7hp and the licence, which costs £3.3/- should be taken out on receipt of the car, and remains in force until 1st January following. The usual male servant's licence (15/-) has to be taken out for a paid driver."

In the 1920s, with cars still outnumbered by carriages on the roads, the chauffeur and engine were often regarded as replacements for the horse. *The Saturday Book* reported: "Apart from the enclosed limousine with division between chauffeur and passengers, there were two popular body styles on expensive chassis. One was the landaulette, in which the rear portion of the roof folded down to give fresh air in fine weather, the ideal car in which to be seen in the park . . . The other body style, more popular in Paris than in London, was the *sedanca de ville*, in which the chauffeur sat in the open, ahead of a limousine or landaulette style of passenger compartment."[4]

The development of aeroplane engines during World War One ("the war to end all wars") had acted as a spur to technological advance and, after watching a friend die from the effects of cranking his car, the American manufacturer Henry C Leland, made life a great deal simpler for the motorist by inventing the electric starter. In 1912 Cadillac pioneered electric lighting and other manufacturers rapidly followed suit. Electric horns were introduced, followed by electric windscreen wipers. It was now time to concentrate on finesse. An early advertisement for Chrysler pictured a new model in front of the Pont du Gard, the

Roman aqueduct near Nimes in France, with text comparing the two and a headline proclaiming "A Wealth of Strength Beneath Its Classic Beauty."

Europe had the edge in the luxury car stakes. One Marc Birkigt, a Swiss largely forgotten by posterity, working at a factory in Barcelona, produced for the Paris Salon of 1919 a masterpiece of mechanical engineering often nominated, even today, as the greatest car of all time. This was the 37.2 horsepower Hispano-Suiza, which weighed in at more than two tons but could achieve speeds of up to 80mph.

British auto expert Colonel JR Buckley, wrote of it in 1960: "This lovely big 6-cylinder engine was unquestionably years ahead of its time. It... was constructed almost entirely of light alloys... The complete upper half of this most beautifully finished motor-car engine was rendered corrosion proof by a closely guarded and patented process of enamelling under pressure. It was one of the finest examples of precision engineering ever made in the field of automobile manufacture... Features of the design would be considered advanced today, though in this day and age the cost of producing such a motor car would be absolutely prohibitive, but to give some small idea of the standards of workmanship which went into it, the massive circular seven-main bearing crankshaft was machined and polished all over; it was machined from a solid billet of the very finest steel procurable, weighing in the rough 770 lb. The finished shaft – and finished it was to a jeweller's degree of accuracy – weighed 99 lb. A mere detail if you please but 671 lb of the finest steels available was machined away to produce this perfect shaft."[5] They most definitely do not make them like that anymore! The Hispano-Suiza – later produced in France – stayed in vogue until the mid 1930s, though very much a rich man's plaything.

As was the Italian Isotta-Fraschini, it's principal competitor. Raymond Chandler described one of these in *The Smell of Fear* as "an open phaeton, huge even for the calculated swank of Hollywood. It glittered like a Ziegfeld chorus as it passed the entrance lights, then it was dull and silver. A liveried chauffeur sat behind the wheel as stiff as a poker, with a peaked cap cocked rakishly over one eye." Rudolf Valentino owned one. So too did Douglas Fairbanks, Ramon Novarro, Mary Pickford and world heavyweight champion Jack Dempsey.

But perhaps the most extravagant cars of this 'golden age' were those made by Ettore Bugatti. The Bugatti Type 41 Royale cost £5,250 – for the chassis alone. Bugatti made only seven Royale Victorias in 1931. As a consequence it is considered the rarest car in the world. The water-cooled, eight cylinder, 12,760cc engine could achieve speeds of up to 125mph, despite the fact that the car weighed three tons. Fuel consumption left something to be desired, however. It did just six miles to the gallon.

Such excess could not last. Mass production of Fords, Morrises and Austins soon made motoring a middle class phenomenon. In his introduction to a 1920s booklet commissioned by the Austin car company, Edward J Burrow, eulogised, "The freedom of the open road – what a glorious prospect is bound up in that simple phrase and all that it means to the lover of adventure! The Austin brings the whole of the country within easy reach of one's door, and laughs at the hills and valleys that lie between us and our once-distant friends. A 25-mile run after tea, a round of golf, or a little tennis, or a quiet talk and home again before dark is an easy venture in the long summer evenings. In anticipation, one thrills with the expectation. I envy you the delightful sensation you will experience when, the last strap having been adjusted on the luggage grid, and a final look at the map, the starter rushes the engine into life, the friends standing at the door of the old home wave a cheery goodbye, and the Austin moves out through the gateway into the venture land of castles and mountains and placid flowing rivers, lakes, waterfalls, swelling moorlands..." Pictures from the 1920s show middle class families seated on blankets a short distance from their trusty Austin, Morris or Ford, enjoying picnics or cups of tea in pristine countryside.

Still more people were introduced to motoring by the 'baby' car – the Austin Seven and the Trojan joined towards the end of the decade by the Singer Junior, the Triumph Super Seven and the Clyno Nine. In America a precursor to the motorway, the four-lane Bronx River Parkway, was completed in 1923.

Times were changing rapidly. By the 1930s the Depression was starting to bite and chauffeurs and ultra-expensive cars were going rapidly out of fashion. The emphasis was now firmly on the mass produced small car. The result was rapidly reflected in official statistics. During the 1920s and 30s, the total number of mechanically propelled vehicles on the roads of Britain increased from one million to well over three million, and the number of private cars from 300,000 to more than two million – by 1938, 2.4 million car licences were in force. At the same time lorries replaced horse-drawn vans and started to challenge the role of the railways as a means of long distance transport. Traffic jams arrived, particularly on roads around seaside resorts at weekends. This was because the roads were far too small for the numbers of cars suddenly using them. In the US, the model for the freeways of the future was established by the Pennsylvania Turnpike; a four-lane highway built on the wide, almost flat bed of an abandoned railroad track. Work started in 1937 and the turnpike was finished in 1940.

Elsewhere in the world, despite the traffic jams that sometimes developed, the car remained very much a symbol of freedom, pictured as helping city dwellers to get back to nature. Advertisements for the Austin Seven showed happy families staring enthralled from clifftops, their car glistening in the foreground – reflecting days when motoring still exuded a definite sense of innocence and adventure. Rodney Dale, author of a book on vintage motoring, now living in Haddenham, near Ely in Cambridgeshire, recalls how in 1939 at the age of five, he and his best friend Mickey were driven "all over East Anglia and points north" in Mickey's father's Wolseley. "Mickey and I... were introduced to the wonders of places as far flung as Bedford, Grantham, and Norwich." Dale recalls how Mickey had a primitive go-kart, in those days described as a 'trolley', and how – unconsciously copying Chinese experiments conducted nearly five millennia previously – they once fitted a sail to it. On a day in which the winds were whipping in off the flat Fenland surrounding Cambridge, they took it for a trial run in the streets near their home. The result probably explains Chinese abandonment of the idea. "I still have the scars," Dale reported.[6]

Around this time, the idea of motoring for the masses became a political ideal. Henry Ford promised "a car in every garage"; while in Germany Adolf Hitler said "every member of the German people" should be a car owner. Motoring was lauded in glowing terms by the Führer, laying the foundation stone for what was to be, for a while, the largest car factory in the world. "It is the young who succumb to this magic. They experience the triumph of the motorcar with the full temperament of their impressionable hearts," he eulogised. "It must be seen as a sign of the invigorating power of our people that they give themselves with such fanatic devotion to this invention, an invention which provides the basis and structure of our modern traffic."[7]

Since the 1923 Munich putsch, Hitler had been a friend of car maker Jakob Werlin of Daimler-Benz. Now, promising the ideal of a *motorisierte Volksgemeinschaft* (motorised populace), he began building the autobahns, the world's first interlocking motorway system. The first motorway (meaning a lengthy stretch of road reserved for motor traffic, with split-level intersections) was actually built in 1925 in Italy by Hitler's ally, the Fascist dictator Benito Mussolini – linking Milan with the Alpine lakes. Mussolini's autostrade formed part of the dictator's economic vision in which industry and state would work together to accelerate national growth. By 1939 seven Italian motorways had been built. By now Hitler had made up for lost time, opening the Cologne-Bonn autobahn in 1932, and within a decade completing more than 2,107 kilometres of motorway in Germany. The British Road Federation was hugely impressed and in 1934 invited Ministry of Transport officials to take a look as the work progressed. The Ministry wisely declined.

Hitler was enchanted by cars. Classic Third Reich propaganda films picture Aryan blondes sitting alongside clean-cut, purposeful male drivers, bowling along in bright sunshine down the revolutionary long, straight roads to the brave new, blond, blue-eyed world of the Führer's stunted imagination.

The British road lobby remained impressed, and in 1937 sent a 255-strong delegation to Germany that included 58 MPs and 54 county surveyors. During the trip they visited the Munich Oktoberfest and observed an historic meeting between two motorway pioneers, Hitler and Mussolini. The British visit represented quite a propaganda coup for Germany. The Road Federation pressed for a British programme of motorway building but the British Ministry of Transport preferred a measured system of road-widening. However in 1938, the

Minister Leslie Burgin visited Germany himself and on his return suggested the building of an experimental British motorway. With war clouds looming, the Treasury had too many defence spending commitments and Burgin's suggestion was vetoed as too expensive.[8] It is a sobering thought that the roots of Britain's present motorway system are to be found in the Third Reich. Hitler also inspired the most successful mass produced car of all time, the Volkswagen Beetle. It was designed in the mid 1930s by Ferdinand Porsche but only put into production after the rebuilding of the bombed-out VW factory in 1948.

The war put paid to motoring for pleasure in Europe and curbed mass production of cars, though petrol driven vehicles were widely used by all the armed forces involved. In Britain the slogan "Is your journey really necessary?" became a national catchphrase, petrol was rationed and there were very few cars on the road. This made them still more romantic for a boy of nine. Rodney Dale recalls: "In 1942, a car breaker's yard was wonderfully exciting – what was thrown out in the name of the war effort would make today's connoisseur drool." At the time, Dale's father was manufacturing handbags and purses. "The point of it for us was the real leather upholstery... You could get a great bundle of otherwise unobtainable leather for ten bob." As his father searched for leather, Dale "was clambering over and exploring derelict vehicles: not only cars, but vans and lorries – and buses, for which I had a special love; there was something majestic about them in their repose, like sleeping elephants. To board a coach with its marvellous smell, that mixture of oil and musty coachwork, which had come all the way from Scotland – still showing the mysterious word 'Oban' on its indicator blind – and to sit in the driver's compartment was absolute magic."[9]

When the war ended Britain voted in a Labour government led by Clement Atlee. Atlee's Transport Minister, Alfred Barnes, is said to have drawn a sketch that he unveiled in the House of Commons tearoom showing his plan for 800 miles of motorway with routes linking the West Midlands with Bristol, Lancashire, London and the North East. But the grim reality was that Britain was virtually bankrupt. Instead, Atlee was forced to embark on an austerity programme, in which domestic consumption would be kept to a minimum and priority would be given to exports. Motoring was greatly curtailed. Tom Swallow, who had been a prisoner of war, returned home in June 1945. "I was fortunate because, being a prisoner of war I was given a fuel allowance when I returned home – so that I could visit my family and old friends – to give me a little bit of freedom. I had the use of the family car, a little Wolseley Hornet, and so one day six of us crowded into it with two or three tents, cooking equipment and food. We set off from Birmingham to Brixham and got just beyond Weston-super-Mare when we got a puncture. Not having a spare, we got in touch with my mother who contacted the Ministry of Transport to obtain a permit for a new tyre. We camped for three days in a farmer's field while we waited! But I was much more fortunate than most. I decided to start a taxi business using the Wolseley with my brother-in-law. I applied for a petrol ration, quoting my prisoner-of-war service and, luckily, was given enough to start the business. I recollect one trip I did from just outside Dudley Castle. Charging half-a-crown apiece, I got home and found I had 12 pieces, which meant I must have 12 passengers in, or on, the little four-seater. But there was no option. There was no other transport. It was either me or they'd have to walk miles and miles."[10]

In 1944 Rodney Dale's father bought the chassis of a 1928 four and a half litre Bentley for £125 and rebuilt the car, using a body that cost him just £5. "My father was a vintage motoring enthusiast in some ways but not in others," Dale says now. "I think he saw the car primarily as a cheap means of transport."[11]

"Petrol was virtually unobtainable, but you could get lighter-fuel if you tried hard." The Bentley's first run was fuelled by a box of "those little squidgy capsules of Ronson lighter fluid." However, "soon after, limited supplies of petrol became available, on ration at 1s 10d per gallon." Even filling the car in conventional fashion was a highly cumbersome business in those days, though young Rodney found it fascinating. "On the top of the Hammond Visible Petrol System was a large calibrated glass vessel containing a vertically-adjustable shower head arrangement. You told the operator how much petrol you wanted, and he moved a lever to raise the showerhead to a height corresponding to a half, 1, 2, 3, 4 or 5 gallons. Then he placed a hand lever on the square of a shaft protruding from the body of the pump, and pumped it back and forth, whereupon petrol started showering out of the head into the glass vessel.

The showerhead contained an overflow pipe so that when the petrol had risen to the preset level it could go no further. Then the nozzle of the hose was unshipped and placed in your petrol tank, and the tap opened, whereupon the contents of the glass vessel emptied into the tank by gravity."[12]

Getting round the petrol ration became something of a national pastime. Victoria Station in London was a good place to go. Car owners went there at dusk, carrying jerry cans to buy petrol from lorry drivers at inflated prices.

Despite all these privations, motoring got underway again. Rodney Dale recalls trips in the Bentley to Newmarket and Ely, both less than 20 miles from Cambridge. "I remember that it seemed to take an interminable time to get there and even longer to get back." Dale's sister Steve recalls picnics on these "rural forays – and they really were rural in those days, even quite close to Cambridge". She says her father bought several other cars and motor cycles which he taxed and insured simply so he could get petrol coupons for their country drives. The number of the vehicle was on the coupon, but as soon as its tank had been filled, the petrol could be siphoned off and put in the Bentley. "In those days, places which we think of today as just a few minutes down the road seemed miles away and it took an awful long time to reach them."[13]

But by now there were very definite harbingers of the problems we are so familiar with in our own age. The traffic jam was a regular fact of life. Rodney Dale recalls, "There were scarcely any by-passes or roundabouts in those days and very few traffic lights. You drove through all the towns and that could sometimes be a dreadfully slow process. And wherever there was a major crossroads between routes going from east to west and from north to south, there would be terrible jams." Doncaster was a particular black spot on the Great North Road. The 20 mile journey from Weston-super-Mare to Bristol on a sunny Sunday could take up to four hours, and on one of the few by-passes that did exist – at Exeter – horrendous jams would develop in summer as people headed for the Devon coast. I personally have memories of these as a small boy sitting on the hot, sweaty leather seats of an old Austin heading, every summer, year in, year out, to Torquay or Paignton on holiday, boot laden with old brown leather suitcases. I think it all seemed a bit boring and aimless to me even then. Rodney Dale too talks about his father's many excursions as "enjoyable enough but rather pointless".

In those days just after the war, the world first licked its wounds, then began heading once more down the road signposted Progress. The British Government's austerity programme, the difficulties of obtaining raw materials and purchase tax of 66.6 per cent on cars selling for over £1,000, initially curtailed the number of vehicles on the roads. In 1948 the basic petrol allowance gave motorists only 100 miles of travel per month – in an economical car. The world was slow to recover from the war and austerity policies were only gradually relaxed. At the same time, the car was a major symbol of freedom for young men with a new life ahead of them after the horrors of the front, and demand outstripped supply. Second-hand cars frequently sold for more than new models, for which there were waiting lists of three or four years. Peter Falconer recalls: "You couldn't get new cars for love nor money, although you could if you were a doctor. In fact doctors would become motor traders, because that's how they could make money."[14]

At the lower end of the social spectrum, the spiv came into his own: classically attired in a black full-length coat with the collar turned up to prevent recognition, a thin moustache, selling fruit from a barrow in the West End by day, 'knocking out' dodgy motors by night.

A degree of legitimacy slowly returned as the world recovered. By 1950 world production of cars totalled 10,017,000. The breakdown was: US, 8,003,000; Britain 783,000; Canada 390,000; France 357,000; Germany 306,000; and Italy 127,000. [15] The British car industry was buoyant, with the Land Rover scoring a great international success and small cars doing surprisingly well in North America. This would change, however, as the French and German motor industries recovered, and the Japanese got in on the act, while Britain became bogged down with strikes and other industrial action.

Cars became more efficient and streamlined, and they were ceremoniously washed and polished on Sundays. Parking restrictions began to arrive and with them the parking meter and that architectural monstrosity, the multi-storey car park. Roads were 'improved' and new ones promised. Road signs began to deface the urban landscape. And as for the humans caught in the middle; very few people stopped to think about it, but society began to be changed by the car and its domination. Perhaps this was some of the "pointlessness" Dale and I felt. From being a great helpmate that had opened up the world for our grandfathers, the car was now aiding and abetting as we lost contact with nature. Is veteran anti-car campaigner Wolfgang Zuckermann going too far when he says: "In one century... a split second of geological time... we have changed the face of the globe from that of a rosy-cheeked young boy to the shrivelled face depicted in the portrait of Dorian Gray"? Consider the world as it was and as it is now. Zuckermann continues: "We have covered the earth with asphalt scars and wrinkles where once were beckoning earth lanes, grassy tracks, and colour – and texture-rich paving stones. What we lost in the process is what the American forester and planner Benton MacKaye 60 years ago called 'connectedness', our direct link to the earth and its landscapes, three of which – city, country and wilderness – he considered to be essential for the maintenance of our psychic health and well-being."[16] Those long, straight roads down which we travel so purposefully hunched over the steering wheels of our cars, like those built by Hitler, may not lead to paradise at all but, far more likely, to the other place.

And I don't mean Felixstowe.

4
FROM THE RAM'S DROPPING BYPASS
TO SPAGHETTI JUNCTION

Alarm bells concerning looming ecological disaster were first sounded in America. Benton MacKaye drew attention to the way modern development was eroding the personality of towns and villages and slowly destroying our "connectedness" with them. MacKaye said a place's personality could be destroyed when just part of it was covered with structures of "individual hideousness and collective haphazardness" to create a "slum of commerce."[1] No prizes for recognising from this description the out-of-town shopping centre or hypermarket. No prizes either for pointing out that no one paid any attention to MacKaye and his theories.

Wolfgang Zuckermann says, "The car's contribution to such landscape deterioration is threefold: first, it is largely responsible for this 'individual hideousness and collective haphazardness' that MacKaye talks about by allowing structures to be scattered about in no particular order with a sea of parked vehicles around them; secondly, and more surreptitiously, it isolates us and speeds us through these very same landscapes so that we lose our distaste for them and they bother us less; and finally, having created the nondescript landscape and having isolated us from it, the car then gives us the means to leave such an area behind and embark on a search for an unspoiled landscape eventually to be blighted in its turn."[2]

Here in the third millennium we may well be so disconnected from nature that the crass ugliness of out-of-town shopping centres and hypermarkets no longer has the capacity to shock. 'Progress' put them there, and there they must stay. Benton MacKaye would doubtless argue that our towns and cities have lost their personalities and our lives have duly been diminished.

And, there is no definitive measure here, but my own feeling is that MacKaye would be absolutely right; that as our environment has lost its identity, so we have lost our "connectedness" and fallen into a certain rootless confusion - though the natural imperative to "keep on the sunnyside" rarely allows us to admit it.

Expressing feelings about our society is something we often leave to poets. In the 1950s, the world was heedlessly and joyfully embarking on a postwar rush towards a 'new' world of peace and plenty, and busy building the roads to take it there. Whether Britain's poet laureate John Betjeman would have heard of Benton MacKaye and his theories is uncertain, but he was nonetheless moved to make a series of films on English towns whose identities he saw as being eroded by the car. One of these was Crewkerne, the small market town in Somerset, where I happened to grow up.

Crewkerne has few claims to fame. One is that the father of Tom Paine, author of the *The Rights of Man*, was born there, though he moved to Norfolk before the birth of his son. Another is that, before the building of the British motorway system, it was for three decades a major bottleneck on the A30 for holidaymakers bound for the coastal resorts of Dorset, Devon and Cornwall. How deep this goes is reflected in Bill Bryson's 1995 bestselling look at Britain, *Notes From A Small Island*. The author describes typical pub directions on how to get from Surrey to Cornwall:

" '– and follow the dirt track through the army firing range and round the back of the cement works, it drops down on the B3689 Ram's Dropping bypass. It saves a good three or four minutes and cuts out the rail crossing at Great Shagging.'

"'Unless, of course, you're coming from Crewkerne,' someone will add eagerly, "Now, if you're coming from Crewkerne . . ."'[3]

After reading Bryson's book, I spent many fruitless hours searching for the *double entendre* in "Crewkerne" (it had, after all, been included with not only the Ram's Dropping bypass and Great Shagging, but also Little Puking, the Buggered Ploughman and Old Toejam). I finally reached the conclusion that there wasn't one; Bryson had probably referred to the town because, even though most holidaymakers can now avoid Crewkerne by using the M5 to the north, he had heard this small, otherwise insignificant place referred to so often, that he realised it was an indelible part of local motoring folklore and would ring a bell with his readers.

As for Betjeman's jerky sepia film on Crewkerne, it filled me with nostalgia. I gazed fondly at the old buildings and shops, the quaint – almost illegible – road signs, the funny old telephone boxes (Remember them? "Push button A, please, caller.") I wondered what on earth Betjeman was going on about in his cultivated lugubrious commentary as he complained about the volume of traffic and the way that cars were ruining the place. The old Triumphs and Austin A-30s rattling by, or parked here and there along the main street, provoked only more nostalgia. In 1951 some 86 percent of Britain's 14.5 million households were without a car.[4] To someone looking back from the third millennium, there was little sign of anything remotely resembling congestion. Yet Betjeman, with a poet's inner eye, divined what was to come. Crewkerne like many other places in modern Britain, has since lost its personality and the car and the way it helps destroy our "connectedness" bears much of the blame.

At least the town has escaped the road-building schemes that have blighted so many other places. When it comes to anger, the car is a moving target, but roads stay in one place and in their construction affect people on a more direct and personal level – by destroying their homes and landscapes they love. And it has been against the roads they run on that the fight against cars has thus far been concentrated. Very few people objected to new roads in the 1950s, of course. Quite the reverse: the world was anxious to forget the horrors and privations of war and cars and new roads led to the future. Yet around the time Betjeman made his film, one of the first modern anti-road protests took place – far far away from Crewkerne and the Ram's Dropping bypass – in New York City. For Wolfgang Zuckermann it marked the start of a lifelong fight against the car.

Now aged 77, Zuckermann recalls, "I was born in Berlin but my parents fled Germany in 1938 so I grew up in New York. What happened was the Park Commissioner, Robert Moses, had the bright idea of building a road through Washington Square Park to relieve pressure on other smaller roads in the area. There was uproar. Local residents united against it. I don't know if there had ever been anything like this before. You must remember that at this time very few people saw cars as a problem, especially in the United States. What we did was quite revolutionary. There were women with children sitting in the road to stop the bulldozers – imagine that in the 1950s! The important thing was that it worked – we stopped the road."[5]

As a result of the protest, not only was the new road halted but an existing street was closed to traffic. "The traffic engineers said there would be chaos but there wasn't. Traffic didn't increase at all as predicted. In fact it declined. Every traffic count taken around the park perimeter and lower Fifth Avenue which led to it showed a slight reduction. Traffic simply disappeared." The Washington Square experience provided an axiom for Zuckermann: build new roads and traffic will inevitably increase, close roads and it will decrease. "We are talking about guerilla warfare here you know," says Zuckermann. He now lives in the southern French city of Avignon, where he runs an English bookshop and still campaigns against the car as a leading light in the local action group *Respirez La Ville* ('Let the Town Breathe').

Back in the 1950s, The Washington Square Park protest was very much the exception to the rule. Road building was to become a major vote-winner for politicians. In 1954 President Eisenhower announced plans for 37,600 miles of interstate highway. This was primarily to stimulate economic growth, but also – in this, the Cold War era – to facilitate the mass evacuation of cities in the event of a nuclear war.

In Britain traffic had increased so much that controls were becoming necessary. In 1954 Winston Churchill's Conservative government produced the Road Traffic Bill, which introduced both roadworthiness tests for cars and parking meters, long a fact of life in American cities. Plans for a motorway network had existed since the war but had been mothballed by Atlee's postwar Labour government (1945-1951). In 1955, an election year, this was dusted off and presented to a nation desperate to escape from its recent past. (That year was also marked by a particularly savage winter, which at one time saw 70 main roads impassable because of snow and ice.) The four year plan would modernise the entire road system with £212 million spent on new motorways and the elimination of traffic blackspots.

The incoming Conservative administration now faced the

problem of funding the motorway plan. Britain had still not shed all the remnants of its Victorian colonial empire and spending on defence remained high. It was only after the Suez debacle in 1956, the nation's last botched attempt at gunboat diplomacy, and the resulting resignation of Prime Minister Sir Anthony Eden the following year, that attitudes changed and cash became available for roads.

Harold Macmillan, who took over from Eden, chose to see Suez as a "tactical defeat". He said, "It is our task to ensure that, like the retreats from Mons and Dunkirk, it should prove the prelude to a strategic victory." That victory would be long-needed cuts in defence and overseas spending, with the emphasis placed firmly on prosperity at home. Macmillan set the seal on his vision at a Conservative rally in Bradford when he compared standards of living with those that prevailed just six years previously and famously proclaimed, "Let's be frank about it. Most of our people have never had it so good." Having it good meant having a car and now motorways would help car owners to have it even better. Macmillan's popularity reached an all-time high. The left wing *Daily Mirror* cartoonist, Vicky, took to portraying the PM as 'Supermac', swooping victoriously through the heavens.

The start to the motorway programme was modest to say the least, wisely made in a part of England containing few traditional Conservative voters and where the countryside no longer mattered, most of it having been ravaged beyond repair since the Industrial Revolution. Preston in Lancashire, part of the inglorious Greater Manchester conurbation, was best known to the rest of the country as a notorious bottleneck. Here cars and trucks heading north to Scotland encountered holiday traffic bound cross country for the delights of the seaside resort of Blackpool, which has more visitors every year than Greece and more holiday beds than the whole of Portugal. (I am indebted to Bill Bryson for those pieces of information. I won't repeat what else he said about the place). Traditionally, Britain is split socially from north to south; the north down-at-heel and unfashionable, the south prosperous and trendy. Historian Corelli Barnett refers to a working class 'tribe apart' in not only the north but South Wales and industrial Scotland.[6] Roy Hattersley, former deputy leader of the Labour Party, turned political pundit, says, "Complaints are not characteristic of the North. Those of us born north of the River Trent – the real dividing line between northern and southern Britain – are always reluctant to admit that we have problems. Even when the difficulties are not of our own making, our instinct is to insist that we need neither help nor comfort. The North, we say, in a typically northern phrase, 'can manage'."[7]

Traffic was so dense at one point just outside Preston, that it is reported that when the long-suffering folk living there wanted to cross the main road, rather than complain, they would frequently 'manage' by catching a bus into the town centre, then another one back out again until they were where they had started from – this time on the other side of the road.

Something obviously had to be done. And to alleviate pressures on the town itself, the Preston bypass, Britain's first motorway, came into being. It was only eight and a half miles long, cost just £4 million and today is an insignificant part of the accident-prone M6. Back in 1957 when it was under construction, it was regarded locally as one of the wonders of the modern world. Each weekend tourists flocked to the site in droves to watch its construction. Macmillan saw it as another vote-winner and, opening it on December 5 1958, hailed "an historic occasion... the opening of a new era of modern travel in the United Kingdom." The Government was determined to push ahead with an imaginative road programme, he said. British Movietone News took a spin along the new road and proclaimed, "This is the shape of Britain to come."

David Bayliss, a transport planner, described driving on the road shortly after it opened: "A friend of mine lent me his V8 Daimler SP 250, which was a wonderful motor car, and driving at 100 miles per hour – because there were no speed limits on motorways in those days – in this beautiful motor car was entirely different from anything I'd experienced before. It was quite special."[8] Local bus services ran trips along it for tourists. Schoolchildren were taken on outings along it. "In my school every class was packed in turn into a chara (charabanc, or coach) and driven down the Preston bypass and back home again. Everyone cheered when you hit a ton," recalls Jean Hudson, a linguist, from Salford. "We never questioned the wisdom of such high speeds. Nowadays, of course, you drive slower if you have children on board."[9] (Elsewhere speed limits were now being backed up by radar checks.)

Stuart Mustow, a civil engineer who became West Midlands county surveyor, said: "Of course, it wasn't very long as a section of road but I remember driving on it and the difference was absolutely tremendous. You had freedom. Suddenly you felt released from all the struggles of having to drive on old trunk roads to the north of the country."[10]

Before we look at what came next – the most shortsighted, shameful and downright shabby episode in the history of transportation and travel in modern Britain – let us pause to recall a few words spoken by Winston Churchill, when he was Chancellor of the Exchequer, in 1928. Not one of the great man's most memorable pronouncements to be sure, but his message was, as always, clear and to the point. "It is the duty of the state to hold the balance between road and rail," he said. Macmillan, infatuated by the success of the Preston bypass, chose not to heed his mentor and the result has been a gradually escalating disaster for Britain.

Looking at newsreel footage, it is easy to see a touch of the music hall comedian about Supermac's Transport Minister, Ernest Marples. But Marples, MP for the Liverpudlian constituency of Wallasey, was actually an extremely astute self-made man who knew exactly which way his bread was buttered. He was one of a new breed of Conservative politicians – representing industry – not one of the "grandees" as Mrs Thatcher would later call the old guard of landed gentry. Marples was a former road engineering contractor and majority shareholder in Marples Ridgway, a leading construction company heavily involved in road building. When he became a minister he officially shed his ties with the firm, but he and his family in fact remained closely connected with it. In his ministerial role, Marples announced plans for 1,000 miles of motorways and as the road building industry geared up for what would be the biggest boom in its history, Marples Ridgway went from strength to strength.

In November 1959 there were 8.5 million vehicles on Britain's roads. Standing on a bridge over the northbound carriageway, Marples opened the country's first full length motorway – the first 72 miles of the M1, linking London with Birmingham. To build this, 20 million tons of earth and gravel had been moved, then five million tons of stone, sand, cement and steel used for foundation, surface and bridgeworks. All of this – heralded as one of "the greatest construction projects in the history of British civil engineering" – was carried out by an army of 5,000 workers – a great many of them Irish, including legendary navvies with nicknames like 'Sullivan The Bull', 'Doyle The Horse' and 'Elephant John'. A qualification for work was a chest that was "40 inches from tit to tit".[11] Because it would later be extended to Leeds, the motorway was initially known as 'the London-Yorkshire highway'. As such, it was lauded by Ewan MacColl, Peggy Seeger and Charles Parker in *Song of a Road*, a melange of songs, instrumental music, sound effects and the recorded voices of those involved in its construction. The M1 was seen by these radical young folk singers in a very non-critical, almost euphoric light.[12] In general, while there had been a few protests, including the daubing of "Marples Must Go" slogans on some bridges, the public was generally supportive of both the road and its creator. Like the Preston bypass before it, the M1 was seen as a very obvious vote-winner. "This motorway starts a new era in road travel," said Marples, echoing Supermac, "It is in keeping with the bold, exciting and scientific age in which we live."

For a while, unlikely as it may seem today, the M1 was part of 'swinging' Britain. Charles Forte's motorway snack bar at Newport Pagnell, forerunner to today's services, became quite trendy. Suzanne Greaves recalled: "This cosy man-made island called out to Britain's youth, the generation of teenagers who did not know there was anything special about being young but forsook the coffee bars of Soho to spend Saturday night 'doing a ton' on this long, straight road. Girls called Brenda, Iris and June – and me – perched on the bar stools of the cream and red snack-bar, patting beehive hairstyles and sipping shilling beakers of Cona coffee with fresh cream… From the steamed-up windows of the snack-bar you could watch the Bentleys and the Rolls-Royces streaming into the car park. Out of them stepped cult figures like singer Tom Jones, the Beatles, the Rolling Stones and the cast of Coronation Street, all heading for the up-market Grill and Griddle."[13] Mrs Gladys Pell worked there as a counter assistant, earning £8 a week. "I remember the Beatles," she recalled, "They were very unruly and threw bread rolls at their manager, Mr Epstein. We had to put them in the Grill restaurant annexe, along with Mick Jagger, because their fans would mob them. Customers would queue for hours just to get a seat and the Grill waitresses were the envy of us all... We saw the first miniskirt here."[14]

By the time the M4 from London to Bristol was built, there was protest but this was muted and splintered, having little effect nationally. In the main, it came from groups such as the Ramblers Association, the Faringdon branch of the National Farmers' Union, the Berkshire branch of the Council for the Preservation of Rural England, the Vale of White Horse Preservation Society and the Downs Preservation Society.

Marples was riding high. Cushioned by his success, he now went one dubious step too far; masterminding a plan that would effectively run down Britain's extensive railway network and allow road transport to take over.

In view of his ties with the road construction industry, it seems fair to speculate on his motives. David Henshaw, author of an exhaustive study of the butchering of Britain's railways, says: "In a few short years, the road interests had become sufficiently powerful to influence political events, making it virtually impossible for the government, or any future government, to hold out against them. From this viewpoint, the question of whether there was, or was not, a conspiracy to crush the railways and who might, or might not, have been involved, becomes irrelevant. The road transport machine, once it had gathered momentum, was to destroy every obstacle in its path. Whether it began to move on its own accord – or was pushed – is no longer important. It would be wrong to suggest that Marples deliberately made political decisions for personal gain, yet with the best will in the world, he would have been unable to make fair and reasoned judgments on transport affairs and he should never have been allowed to try."[15]

Henshaw says now: "I think when you look back today, you have to grant that these people really thought at the time they were doing the right thing for the country. They thought that motorways were essential for its welfare and that railways were old fashioned. History was to prove them wrong. Their decisions were a tragedy for Britain."[16]

The railways had been nationalised by the Labour administration that came to power after the war in 1945, after which they had been appallingly badly run. They were hugely overstaffed, made enormous losses and were bedevilled by strikes. In 1962, a year in which their deficit topped £160 million after interest, Marples appointed Dr Richard Beeching, technical director of the chemical company ICI, to head the British Transport Commission at a salary of £24,000, giving him *carte blanche* to make British Railways efficient.

While it is true that something needed to be done to improve the efficiency of the railways, the trouble with *The Reshaping of British Railways*, the report that Beeching produced on March 27 1963, was that he threw the baby out with the bathwater. Beeching stunned the nation by calling for the rail network to be slashed by a quarter, with the closing of 2,128 stations and the shedding of 67,700 jobs. There would be no passenger services north of Inverness, and most branch lines in north and central Wales and the West Country would be axed. Seen from the perspective of the transport problems afflicting Britain today, what Beeching proposed was an act of vandalism on the grand scale, one that would leave the country with no viable land-based alternative to road transport and which completely ignored the needs of people living in isolated communities.

TW Jones, MP for Meirionydd, said angrily (and rather incoherently) at the time, "Dr Beeching's report has proved to be the most staggering report ever presented to any government... He has closed the railways. If I stopped a train, I would be fined £5. Dr Beeching stops a third of the railway system and gets a cheque for £24,000... On the law of averages, as I should be fined £5, the Minister should be deported."[17]

In 1990, Robert Adley, who was Conservative MP for the now defunct constituency of Bristol North East and a great rail enthusiast, could look back more in sadness than anger: "Beeching did more than close railway lines: he affected attitudes to the railway which, unfairly and unfortunately persist to this day." Reflecting on the Beeching Report from an age in which roads were choked with cars and juggernauts, Adley asked, "Who could have then foreseen, as many indeed have not even yet foreseen, that the form of 'motive power' that was responsible for the assault on and the near demise of the passenger railway, namely the internal combustion engine, may yet become the *raison d'être* of its renaissance?" Adley, like many other rail advocates, questions the figures Beeching and other 'experts' used to assess transport costs. "What chance is there of a full and honest cost-benefit analysis as between road and rail? How does one assess the 'cost' of death, for example? Roads gobble up infinitely more land; cost much more to build; generate immeasurably more pollution and congestion; kill and maim countless tens of thousands; create untold costs for the National Health Service; involve millions of hours of time for police and courts annually; and have virtually everything funded by the taxpayer... The railway, in terms of cost/benefit to the nation, scores endlessly on such comparisons."[18] How sad no one could see it this way back in the early 1960s.

Times were changing. Industrial unrest was escalating, with car workers leading the way. The Profumo scandal broke. Any postwar optimism that still existed evaporated rapidly, and a new and more cynical mood settled over the British. Macmillan was one of the first casualties. Historian Kenneth O Morgan observes: "He changed almost dramatically, from the dominant, unflappable Supermac of Vicky's half-admiring cartoons to the fading Edwardian caricature of the Profumo scandal, an antiquated poseur, the ready butt for university satirists, the grouse moor image come to life. When in October 1963 he was succeeded by a fourteenth earl (Sir Alec Douglas-Home as he renamed himself) who confessed that he worked out economic problems by the use of matchsticks, derision knew no bounds."[19]

Things were looking up for Labour. Its leader Harold Wilson, under pressure from his left wing and the rail unions, had agreed to halt the rail closures proposed by Beeching pending a national transport survey. But duplicity is the prerogative of politicians once they are in power, at which time it becomes known instead as 'pragmatism'. During the Labour party conference of 1963, Wilson came out with his most famous soundbite: "We are redefining our socialism in terms of the scientific revolution... The Britain that is going to be forged in the white heat of this scientific revolution will be no place for restrictive practices or outdated methods on either side of industry." He stopped short of referring to the rail industry (which was riddled with restrictive practices), but there can be no doubt that he saw the future as belonging to the motorways and air transport. One way or the other, once the 1964 election was won, Wilson forgot his pledge and Beeching's draconian closures continued.

By the mid-1960s, as the railways closed, hundreds of miles of motorway were under construction, and the face of the country was being irrevocably changed. In those days it was rare to find anyone with even the slightest pang of conscience over the damage done. Brian Behan, who worked on the construction of several motorways recalled, "One minute you'd reach a great big hill and the next minute you'd see the old JCBs, the drag lines, tearing the heart out of the hill. And before you knew where you were, you were through the hill. And that seems to me a most marvellous accomplishment."[20]

The cruel fact of the matter concerning the "marvellous accomplishment" was that Britain's motorway building programme was carried out on the cheap. The winter after the Preston bypass was opened, it froze over and, ominously, parts of it collapsed. John Cox, project manager for the bypass said, "We didn't cut corners. We built it in accordance with the requirements but sadly they were inadequate."[21] All the other motorways had similar flaws but the cracks would take a while to appear and, despite the hiccough with the Preston bypass, the new roads were still seen as symbols of the future.

And it came to pass that in the white heat of Wilson's scientific revolution, the planners decreed that Birmingham – Britain's second city in the industrial West Midlands – would become the country's 'motorway city'. The majority of the citizens of Birmingham – a place of decaying red brick terraced housing and industrial smokestacks – latched onto the dream, thinking their living conditions would improve as a result. They were told that motorways, raised on concrete pillars to cut right across the city, would regenerate the region, improve communications with the rest of the country and attract industry. At the same time slums would be demolished. A city official can be seen in old newsreel, exclaiming euphorically, "I'm hoping and I believe it will be true that Birmingham will be one of the most beautiful cities in Europe when this redevelopment job is completed."

The job has long ago been completed and we can look at this vision with the advantage of hindsight. Let us compare the Birmingham of our 21st century with France's second city, Lyon. Both conurbations occupy a central location in their respective countries and are built at junctions for waterborne traffic: Birmingham at a major linking point of the old British canal system, Lyon where the mighty rivers Rhone and Saône meet. Both are now hubs for motorway traffic, and both have been extensively redeveloped. Today only one is by any stretch of the imagination one of the most beautiful cities in Europe. Birmingham it isn't.

To be fair, Lyon suffered its share of civic vandalism and motorway madness. Under Louis Pradel, mayor of the city from 1955-1976, a disastrous programme of modernisation was started. It was one that resulted in the destruction of several *quartiers* of fine period buildings and the boring of a tunnel through the Fourvière Heights, which dominate the city, to accommodate the main north-south French motorway. For years Lyon was notorious for the traffic jams that built up in this tunnel. But with Pradel out of the way, it was admitted that a mistake had been made: the A46 ring road was built around the edge of the city to take through-traffic, with links to other motorways going north, south, east and west and to the local airport, Satolas. Lyon itself, spared the noise and fumes of thousands of cars daily, enjoyed a renaissance, rediscovered by more and more of those people who had hitherto just driven through it or – more likely – had sat fuming impotently in Pradel's Fourvière tunnel. The old town, France's first urban conservation area, has been immaculately restored, its cobbled streets bordered by small restaurants and boutiques. It is an oasis of calm amid the hustle and bustle of the modern city. Veronique Charpenet, a press relations officer for the city, says, "We are not envious of Parisians. Our quality of life is far superior. In Paris you can spend two hours simply getting to work in the mornings. Life there is stressed and hurried. We know how to live in Lyon."[22]

Today, when comparisons are made with mainland European cities, the most that can be, and often is, said of Birmingham (usually with a rather nasty, condescending snigger) is that it has more miles of canal than Venice.

However, the city does boast one major European landmark, though it is one that no one wants to talk about nowadays. Many of Birmingham's canals merge at a place called Gravelly Hill, just outside the city. Today these are dwarfed by an awesome engineering feat that is a terrifying example of what happens when cars impose their logic on a city, rather than vice versa. Gravelly Hill is the site of Spaghetti Junction. Built on 600 concrete columns and spread over 30 acres, this is Europe's most complex motorway interchange, with 18 routes merging on six levels. The building of Spaghetti Junction required 250,000 tons of concrete. It was necessary to clear housing, and to divert a river and a canal. Steve Cemm, a land surveyor who worked on the M6, says, "When we drive down to Cornwall, we often stop and look at the view over the Tamar bridge and we look and there it says 'Isambard Kingdom Brunel' in big letters over the railway bridge. We look at the suspension bridge and marvel at it. Now we're driving through Spaghetti Junction who remembers the designers, the people who did this? It's just as much an achievement. In fact to my mind, it's even more of an achievement." Stuart Mustow says, "At the time, people said, 'This is the sort of thing you see in the States.' It all went with being a Brummie, it all went with what we need in this place, to make this place count and I think people were proud of it in a funny sort of way."[23]

From Spaghetti Junction motorways cut right across Birmingham, dominating the city. Today that 1960's vision of the future is simply dehumanising dust, fumes and noise. When I drove through the city, heading for a day out at the Wolverhampton races, in the mid 1990s, I was horrified to hear police sirens and see young children playing on the hard shoulder of the M6, as cars and lorries thundered by a short distance away. When the roads were built, Birmingham was remarkably quiescent. There were no objections because as Bob Dylan put it (albeit in a somewhat different context), "When you've got nothin', you've got nothin' to lose". Steve Cemm recalls, "We found that when we went along and said, 'Can we survey? Can we go in your gardens?' far from rejecting us, these people welcomed us. They gave us tea, they gave us cakes. We couldn't at first understand why we were so well treated but it became obvious that they saw the motorway as their route out.

The motorway was going to come, their homes were going to be taken away and they would be rehoused somewhere better." [24]

The British Midlands are a nondescript, unlovely halfway house – an uncomfortable, unfashionable hinterland located only just south of the great divide marked by the River Trent. Like Preston, Birmingham was a pushover for the planners. It would be a different story when they turned their attention to the shires of southern England where power traditionally resides. No cups of tea and slices of cake awaited the surveyors there.

5

TYME TURNS THE TIDE

A disastrous devaluation of the pound and a round of debilitating strikes left British industry, and in particular car companies, reeling. However, the mood in the mid 1960s was upbeat: Bobby Moore led the national football team to win the World Cup, and the Beatles dominated the global pop charts. Things could still go Britain's way and – heady with euphoria – the planners at the Department of Transport set course for Utopia. They used the department's formidable array of computers to process facts and figures, calculate trends and project traffic growth. Plans for motorways and other road schemes were drawn up to meet these needs. The process was called 'Predict and Provide'. Transport planner David Bayliss explains, "The philosophy of 'Predict and Provide' meant that you calculated what the demand for travel would be at some date in the future, then simply designed the capacity to accommodate that."[1] It all sounded so rational and easy. Civil engineer Stuart Mustow says he felt he was "on the cutting edge of something new for Britain." He said, "There was a tendency among professionals at the time to feel that everything was possible. Here you had the tools that made it possible to be pretty certain what the future was going to be."[2]

Nothing was allowed to get in the way of this planned dream world. True, Britain was a democracy and by law there had to be public inquiries into road schemes, and the public was notoriously fickle and might object. But this eventuality had been catered for. The inquiries were run by the government and were heavily weighted in favour of the Department of Transport. An inspectorate panel of the Lord Chancellor's department selected inspectors to chair the inquiries, most of them former civil servants who were required to give no proof of impartiality. The inquiries gave an *impression* of democracy, while in fact merely rubber stamping road schemes.

David Widdicombe QC says, "Our public inquiry system works well enough when the proposal under investigation is promoted by a local authority or private developer – that is, someone other than the Government. But as applied to Government sponsored projects like motorways it is thoroughly unsatisfactory. This is partly because the Government combines the roles of advocate for the scheme and judge of the objections to it, compounding this unfairness by appointing as inspectors at the inquiries persons such as ex-civil servants who do not strike the public as independent. Far more important, though, is the embargo placed at the inquiry on all discussion on the main thing everyone wants to discuss, namely whether the project should take place at all."[3]

As far as the planners and the road builders were concerned, such objectors were not worth the time of day. Alan Whitfield, civil engineer at the Department of Transport from 1970 to 1980 says, "If anyone who was aggrieved by a road said, 'I would like to question the total need of this road', we said, 'I'm sorry, Mr. Inspector, that's outside the scope of this inquiry. 'Need' is not to be debated. That's a policy of the Department of Transport.' We spent a lot of time – I think rather sadly – not explaining things properly to people and unfortunately when we got objections, we just poured all our technical arguments, all the talent that we had, into rebutting those arguments because we believed what we were doing was right. Now, in retrospect, some of those roads were in the right place, some of them weren't, but in those days it was head down and bottom up and get the road done."[4]

Such manifest injustice might have persisted unchecked but for the arrival on the scene in the early 1970s of one of those marvellously awkward, nonconformist characters that, seemingly, only English society – with its deep schisms – can create. The name of this unsung modern folk hero is John Tyme. Here was a campaigner for justice who by force of his blazing-eyed idealism, perspicacity, and persistence set in train a course of events that would save great tracts of the country from going under concrete.

David Widdicombe, qualifying his remarks on the public

inquiry system, said: "One does not have to agree with everything John Tyme has said and done to recognise the important service which he and his supporters have performed in opening up to scrutiny and debate the whole subject of decision-making in the field of Government-sponsored projects."[5]

John Tyme is not the easiest person to interview. When I met him, he was 75 but still as feisty and combative as he ever was. "The details of my life are not important," he said, fixing me with a stern eye. "Concentrate on the issues. It's the issues that are important."

Nonetheless, I winkled a few biographical details out of him. Tyme was born in Sheffield and grew up in one of the city's south-west suburbs, near the Peak District. This National Park is one of the most lovely and unspoiled regions of northern Britain; 542 square miles of rolling green hills, heather and peat moors, grit stone ridges and tumbling, clear rivers. Tyme recalls growing up imbued with a deep love of the countryside: "I had a 3,000 acre wood right on my doorstep and I would play there as a boy. It was quite marvellous. Betjeman once said of Sheffield, that although it was a major industrial city, it possessed some of the leafiest suburbs in the whole of Britain and, believe me, that is no exaggeration. I could walk out from the cottage where I lived and in just three minutes, less, be in some of the most glorious countryside in England."[6]

Tyme's father was a butcher and many of his family were farmers. He has been a member of the Labour Party all his adult life, though his anti-roads campaigning was always resolutely apolitical.

Looking back on his childhood, he says, "I hardly went near the centre of Sheffield when I was a boy. Most of my life was spent in the country." At school he was "regrettably" never any good at maths or science, and went on to take a degree in history at the Scottish university of St. Andrew's. On graduation, he became a teacher at the Royal Academy in Inverness. Tyme married and fathered three daughters but the marriage ended in divorce. In 1955 he left Britain to teach English in the Sudan. "I was in the Sudan for what is now seen as a golden period in that country's history," he says. "This lasted basically from independence to the arrival of Islamic militancy." In his spare time he travelled around the country and on one occasion met

Lord Kitchener's suffragi, or servant. He began painting in oils, in a bold red and ochre palette that he says is the way the land looks at sunset. One picture shows two women, one Arab, the other a Dinka from the south, standing in an embrace. "I didn't think of it when I painted it, but it seemed to me when I looked at it later that what I was trying to do subconsciously was express a desire that the north and the south could find a way of living peacefully together," he says. He obviously revelled in the unspoilt nature of the Sudan. "There were no proper roads there when I arrived and none when I left. I used to say to members of the British road lobby, 'Why don't you go to the Sudan if you want to build roads?'"

Tyme's return to England in 1968 coincided with a severe depletion of national optimism as Harold Wilson's Chancellor, Roy Jenkins, produced the most severely deflationary budget since the war. Historian Kenneth O Morgan says, "Instead of stop-go, it would be stop-stop."[7] Tyme was appointed senior lecturer in environmental studies at Sheffield Polytechnic (now Sheffield Hallam University). Far more fatefully, he became a member of the Conservation Society, a once prestigious environmental organisation made defunct by the growth of more dynamic groups such as Friends of the Earth and Greenpeace.

By the late 1960s, road building was starting to be seen as a major environmental issue. Following their 'success' in Birmingham, the civil engineers had turned their attention to London with plans for a three-tier system of motorways leading out from the centre. Plans for what was called the London Motorway Box had been supported by the Conservative-led Greater London Council in the early 1960s, and by the Labour administration that followed in 1966. "This was the era when Labour believed in 'technology' to solve all Britain's problems: and the 'Motorway Box' which had been handed to them on a plate was technology with a vengeance," said one commentator.[8] The plans sparked the first real anti-roads protests in Britain. Nick Lester, a former transport campaigner, recalls, "As the real scale of the proposals were published and the first sections were built, and people saw just how close houses would be and just how many homes would have to be demolished, the idealism or Utopian vision of the future faded."[9] Instead, concern became focused on the people affected.

One of the most high profile of these was the eminent child psychologist Anna Freud. She discovered that the route for the so-called North Cross motorway passed through the middle of her home in Hampstead, opposite The Child Therapy Course and Clinic of which she had been director since 1952. As she tried to explain to the planners, her real worry was that if the scheme went ahead the study used by her father Sigmund, founder of modern psychology, would be lost to posterity. Freud had worked there after fleeing from the Nazi regime in Austria in 1938.

Elections to the Greater London Council gave the protesters a platform. Terence Bendixson, who was involved in the fight, recalls, "A group of us had this idea that if virtually every borough in London had standing in it council candidates called Homes Before Roads candidates, we could get media exposure and in that way dominate the election with this issue of the ring roads. We didn't expect to be elected. We wanted to be on the front pages. We wanted the ringways to be the No 1 election issue. Electorally speaking, it was a fiasco. We were a complete disaster. But politically speaking, we showed what unbelievable destruction the engineers were planning and I don't think up till then the politicians realised this."[10] The road known as Ringway Two was scheduled to pass through the home in Norbury, South London, of Peter Walker, a young political researcher. He wrote and delivered a manifesto to the GLC that resulted in the abandonment of this road. Only parts of the London Box, such as the West Way, were ever built (and Freud's study was saved from demolition). The incoming Labour council scrapped what remained of the scheme.

Meanwhile back in Sheffield, John Tyme took up the Green cause. "I had arrived back to find that the environment was very much on the social and political agenda. My first foray in this direction was to protect the wood I played in as a child. I managed to stop development there."

He and other campaigners were spurred on by the establishment of Friends of the Earth in England in 1971, and such rallying cries as *The Ecologist* magazine's Blueprint for Survival published in 1972. It succinctly stated the green case: "The principal defect of the industrial way of life with its ethos of expansion is that it is not sustainable. Radical change is both necessary and inevitable because the present increases in human numbers and *per capita* consumption, by disrupting ecosystems and depleting resources, are undermining the very foundations of survival."[11]

After his two forays, Tyme's remarkable 'career' as a thorn in the side of the roads programme gathered pace. Ask him for his motivation and with the curt instruction "It's all in the book", he refers you to the following passage from his book *Motorways versus Democracy*: "It is my belief, and one shared by increasing numbers of people, that the motorway/trunk road programme with all its ramification poses a consummate evil, and constitutes the greatest threat to the interests of this nation in all its history. None of our national enemies have so mutilated our cities, undermined the long-term economic movement of people and goods, destroyed our industrial base, diminished our ability to plan our community life, and reduced our capacity to feed ourselves. The more highways we build, the more we generate traffic to fill them, the greater the congestion and snarlups, and thus the more highways we require to build. The more we build, the more we confirm and perpetuate the horrendous accident level as motorway-generated traffic makes its way onto crowded city and suburban streets. The more roads and motorways built, the more inevitable is the decline of alternative transport modes. The more roads, the greater the housing loss and destruction of community and the less house-building and resources for hospitals, schools and social services. The more highways, the more we are committed to the disaster known as 'dispersal planning' based upon the notion that distance between residence and work, shops and schools, recreation and medical services is no object; and the more dispersal planning, the greater the loss of land and agricultural production. The more resources we commit to road transport, the more we create social inequity, as well over 40 per cent of households who do not own a car and are now never likely to, are left unable to pay the rising cost of public transport, simply watching the cars and juggernauts go by."[12]

The question Tyme now had to ask himself was how on earth he could fight the motorways when the public inquiry system was weighted so heavily in favour of the Transport Department. "Very early on I realised that the inquiry system was so designed to ensure that not only were objectors bound hand and foot, they were also blindfolded and deafened," he says. "In other words, there was no possibility of opposing a road scheme as the inquiries then stood. So it occurred to me that the only way to bring about any real change was to block the inquiries from ever taking place and thus secure sufficient national attention, the concern of Parliament, the concern of Government for the manifest corruption of the whole planning process that was going on."[13]

After attending an inquiry into the M42 at Bromsgrove, Tyme "cut his teeth", as he puts it, at the inquiry into the building of the M40 motorway in 1973 at Kenilworth, West Midlands. Here he addressed the Inspector, Major General RCA Edge with great eloquence: "Sir, you hold an honourable rank, historic predecessors of yours were once addressed by The Protector in the following words, 'Have account unto the common weal'. The proposal before you is that of the great and powerful of this world. Part of my submission is that likewise you take account of those lesser people whom the Conservation Society seeks to represent." Tyme's normally severe features relax into a smile and he confesses, "The only trouble was Oliver Cromwell never said any such thing!"

He asked Edge to adjourn the inquiry because the Department of Transport had produced no information on the need for the motorway. "When the inspector refused, I recall slamming down the lid of my case and saying that, to show our contempt, for these improper proceedings, we would walk out. Which we did. It was a very quiet affair, but significantly BBC national TV had come at my request; we walked straight out upon running cameras, and there followed the first television interview. It could be said that battle had been joined."[14]

Publicity was vital for anti-roads campaigners. When Otmoor, an area of marshland near Oxford, was threatened by the M40, Joe Weston, a member of Friends of the Earth, divided the land into tiny packages that were sold to protestors in order to block compulsory purchase. The stunt attracted headlines.

By 1974 even *The Archers*, a conservative BBC radio soap that bills itself "an everyday story of country folk", was starting to feature ecological issues. Tom Sharpe's novel *Blott on the Landscape*, published the following year, mocked the whole motorway controversy. It featured a Tory MP with a penchant for sado-masochism and bondage who is out to make millions from the construction of a motorway through property owned by his horrendous aristocratic wife. Blott, a former German prisoner-of-war who works as a gardener on the estate, finally saves the day. One piece of dialogue aptly sums up the British system of public consultation on government projects. A senior civil servant informs one of his juniors: "When you have been in public service as long as I have you will know that Inquiries, Royal Commissions and Boards of Arbitration are only set up to make recommendations that concur with decisions already taken by the experts."[15]

Truth was in many ways much stranger than fiction, as Tyme's one-man anti-roads crusade continued apace. By November 1975 under the headline "Halt, major road protester ahead", the *Sunday Times* reported: "John Tyme has an impressive list of battle honours to his name. As Britain's most formidable 'professional' protester against the March of the Motorways and the faceless planners of Whitehall, this 49-year-old Sheffield polytechnic lecturer has fought the following campaigns: M42; M40; M20; M56; M65; M25; M16; and A55 (North Wales).

"Mr Tyme's activities reached a stunning climax last week at the public inquiry into the Aire Valley dual carriageway, a route planned to run through 11 miles of Yorkshire countryside. By organising local protesters into a battalion of shouters, singers, orators, catcallers and even harmonica players, he disrupted proceedings for six turbulent days, finally forcing the ministry inspector in charge to admit defeat and adjourn the inquiry until next month. Sixty protesters were ejected in the course of the action, and 13 others face charges brought by West Yorkshire police.

"Mr Tyme makes no apologies. A graduate of St. Andrew's University in Fife, he quotes the words of a former graduate, the Marquis of Montrose:

He either fears his fate too much
Or his deserts are small
That puts it not unto the touch
To win or lose it all.

Tyme's activities were by now monitored, he says, by the Special Branch. Undaunted, he told Chris Ryder, the *Sunday Times'* reporter: "The fear I have of the Special Branch and a conspiracy charge is nothing to the dread horror that faces this country unless we can break the back of the road lobby and the Department of the Environment." There were other fears, Tyme recalled several years later. "It was at a lunch and I was putting a forkful of food into my mouth and suddenly I heard a road lobby representative who was sitting next to me saying these extraordinary words. He said, 'You know, people like you will find yourself in a Peter Hain situation. You want to be very careful with what you're doing.' Now Peter Hain, MP, had recently then been accused of some theft or other. So I can tell you that the next 48 hours were to me a period of great anxiety. I went to the police in Sheffield and I explained the matter to them and that was taken down in writing and I saw my solicitor and I had a statement put under my carpet in my cottage just in case some woman knocks on the door and starts tearing her clothes off and then screams, then where am I, where's my status at a public inquiry?"[16]

The next round in Tyme's battle came when the Department of Transport unveiled horrific plans for a ten-lane highway, a link to the M3, across the cathedral city of Winchester's historic water meadows. Here, near the village of Sparkford, in the 12th century, legend has it that Henry de Blois, then Bishop of Winchester, met a milkmaid carrying a baby in her arms and a pail of milk on her head. In the hazy light (and perhaps having had a bit of a liquid lunch), Henry thought he was seeing the Virgin Mary wearing her tall crown and carrying the infant Jesus. The milkmaid told him that people in Sparkford were starving and begged him to do something "out of his charity" to help the place. Still impressed by the feeling he had that he had seen the Virgin Mary, Henry set up the Saint Cross almshouse and abbey for 13 poor men of the parish. Workers were paid a penny a day by de Blois to build the almshouse and the children's nursery rhyme, *See Saw, Margery Daw*, dates from this time. In its original form, the chorus went:

See Saw, Messer de Blaw,
Johnny shall have a new master.

He shall get a penny a day
Yet he shan't have to work any faster.

"Messer de Blaw" was how Hampshire workers, or Johnnies, as they called themselves, pronounced "Monsieur de Blois".[17] Like Henry Ford, the planners thought history to be bunk. If their plan for the M3 went ahead, the new superhighway would abut Saint Cross. Winchester was appalled. Initial moves against the scheme were in keeping with the city's ancient and gentlemanly traditions. Its college raised money for an appeal against the plan by asking all old boys to give at least £10 each. It said irreversible damage would be done to the spirit and heritage of the city if the scheme was put into effect. Then, in what *The Times* called "an erudite constitutional move", objectors summoned a meeting of the Commissioners of the Itchen Navigation. They did this by nailing a notice on the Butter Cross in the city and putting advertisements in the *Hampshire Chronicle*. The commissioners, who had not met for a century and a half, had since time immemorial supervised navigation on the Itchen River between Southampton and Winchester. Undeterred by the fact that there had been no navigation on the river since 1869, the objectors exerted their rights under seven acts of Parliament dating back to 1665, arguing that the new highway would indeed greatly impair navigation.

It was all very quaint, but finally it was John Tyme who saved the day and Saint Cross with the kind of civil disobedience Henry de Blois would doubtless have put down by the sword (only to then build another almshouse to appease his guilt). When the inquiry into the M3 plans opened in Winchester Guildhall in July 1976, Tyme orchestrated incredible scenes. Ian Mather reported in the *Observer*: "Normally staid, middleclass people shouted, chanted and stood on their chairs until they forced (the inquiry) to a halt. Tyme is a one-man commando unit whose sniping at the Department of the Environment is so accurate that the Department's position at public inquiries into new road schemes is on the point of becoming untenable. His obsessive passion for the detailed wording of Acts of Parliament and memoranda reduces Ministry officials to helpless apoplexy." Tyme and John Thorn, headmaster of Winchester College, were among more than 100 people ejected by police from the inquiry but they won the day. The water meadows scheme was eventually abandoned, though the affair had a sequel, which we shall come to later.

In September 1976, an *Observer* report on the inquiry into the Archway road scheme in North London contained the following description of Tyme, "The motorway rebels' tactician is a slightly built, highly strung man of 50 with the lean, intense look of a Protestant martyr." The report said Tyme's value to the objectors was "not primarily his statement of their argument – many of them were as articulate as he – not even his tactical advice, but the assurance he gives naturally conformist people by his palpable presence that they are not alone. 'Once you have shouted "No!" in chorus, you will be different people,' he told them."

However, Tyme was devoting so much time to his motorway protests, that there was very little left over for his students at Sheffield Polytechnic. Around the time of the Archway inquiry, he was ordered by the college principal to return. However, the Rowntree Social Services Trust came to his rescue by giving him a grant of £3,000 a year for two years. This enabled him to resign from the Polytechnic, so that he could devote himself to full-time campaigning on environmental matters. A jubilant Tyme told the *Observer* in January 1977: "Opposition to road-building will be coordinated in such a way that every local proposal by the DoE will become national." Tyme now had offices in Poland Street, in London's Soho, which he shared with Friends of the Earth. It was ironic that members of the world's newest profession should choose a part of town more usually favoured by the world's oldest.

Tyme grew still bolder in his approach. In April 1977, at the continued inquiry into the Archway scheme, he told the inspector, the quaintly named Mr Ralph Rolph politely but firmly, "From this moment, sir, this inquiry is occupied." His supporters then unfurled a banner proclaiming "OCCUPATION" and sat cross-legged on the floor. More drama followed. The following month *The Times* reported: "Mr John Tyme, the anti-motorway campaigner, was ejected from a public inquiry at Ipswich yesterday, padlocked to a table. He was appearing at the opening of an inquiry into a by-pass for Ipswich, which would cost £39m. He questioned the validity of the proceedings but his submission was ruled out of order by Mr Frank Clinch, the inspector. When asked to go, Mr Tyme refused and chained and locked himself to the leg of a table. Police officers and officials carried the table from the hall with Mr Tyme attached." Today he smiles wanly at the memory and says, "It was very difficult getting both the table and me into the police van outside. When we got to the police station, I gave them the key, of course."

Attitudes to cars and road-building were by no means clearly defined. In December 1977, the Department of Transport raised the White Flag against what the Press was now calling The Tyme Machine. Its Leitch committee issued a damning report on motorway building. It said many roads had been built in the wrong place, that traffic forecasts had been too high and cost estimates too low. A White Paper following on from this signalled an end of large-scale motorway building in Britain. It promised a more flexible approach with the improvement of roads in phases and to different standards according to need, rather than "building to lines superimposed on maps and to rigid standards."

Plans for Utopia were not working out. Cars themselves – at least domestic models – were going through a bad patch. A number of hitherto famous makes were merged under the British Leyland banner and propped up with taxpayers' money, as cheaper and often better models from elsewhere, notably Japan, began flooding on to the roads.

In 1978 Tyme's book *Motorways Versus Democracy* was published by Macmillan. Though a great campaigner, Tyme was no writer. The book is dry as dust, a gathering together of the papers he had accumulated, reproducing the minutiae of his battle and the discussion *ad nauseam* of procedural and tactical points. Predictably, it was not a huge success and a promised follow-up, *Roads to Ruin*, failed to appear. Looking back on the episode, Tyme sees conspiracy. "Each week I would go along to Macmillan's from my offices in Poland Street to pick up 20 or so copies," he says. "One day I arrived and they told me there weren't any more. I was later told by an editor that they had destroyed a thousand or so copies – by mistake. Then they turned down *Roads to Ruin*."[18]

Brilliant touches of farce continued to pervade his fight. At an inquiry later that year into the M65 Calder Valley motorway, after Tyme had been refused permission to speak, objectors arrived with their children who attempted to play with model cars on the inspector's desk and operate an electric train set on the floor of the hall.

But public and media fatigue with Tyme's campaign was beginning to set in, whilst The Department of the Environment was at long last starting to get his measure. It reformed the procedures for public inquiries into road schemes and – by Tyme's own admission – began handling outbreaks of civil disobedience more intelligently. Two inquiries into the route of the M25 London orbital motorway in the late 1970s attracted minimal national press and television coverage, even though one of these – into the Ashstead-Leatherhead section of the road – saw what Tyme describes as "greater levels of civil disobedience than at any other inquiry."

Tyme says, "Without national reporting, it might just as well never have taken place. In a sense the attitude of the press was understandable. The media thought that with the reforms that had been brought in, there was really no cause for the action, that the inquiries were now legitimate. In fact, of course, nothing of substance had changed." He is backed on this by Tom Burke, special adviser to the Secretary of State for the Environment on "green" issues. Writing more than 20 years after Tyme's campaign, Burke says, "The way in which trunk road planning has been executed in this country is profoundly undemocratic – it gives a pretence of allowing for local objection, but does not give the substance to that." Trunk road planning in Britain involved "the hi-jacking of the political process by a technical elite," said Burke.[19]

John Tyme's name faded from the headlines. He went to live in the Gloucestershire town of Stroud and, when his grant from the Rowntree Trust ran out, pursued what he describes as a 15 year career of "lay advocacy" – representing people at public inquiries. Today, in retirement, he looks back on what he calls "that momentous period" in the mid and late 1970s and remains as involved, passionate, erudite and awkward as ever. He says he has no regrets, and I imagine that no one who ever crossed swords with him, especially all the public inquiry inspectors he reduced to near-apoplexy, would really expect him to have any.

6

MRS T AND
THE "GREAT CAR ECONOMY"

Throughout the 1970s, British politics oscillated uncertainly from left to right and back again; bedevilled by pressure on the pound and wave upon wave of industrial unrest. Much of it centred on the car industry, and in particular the Ford plant at Dagenham. There was now and again speculation that the country was on the verge of becoming ungovernable.[1] As economic and industrial chaos reigned, prime ministers came and went: Harold Wilson, with his pipe and Gannex raincoat; Edward Heath, whose conductor's baton had replaced Sir Alec Douglas Home's matchsticks at the helm of the Conservative party; Wilson again; and then "Sunny" Jim Callaghan who presided over the 'winter of discontent', one filled with strikes and economic misery. It was time for a change, and Margaret Thatcher's election victory in 1979 marked "a decisive shift in the national mood, politically, intellectually and culturally."[2] Thatcher had her own Utopian vision of the future. She dreamed of creating "the great car economy" with out-of-town retail, recreational facilities and business parks – based on the American model.

With output of North Sea oil exceeding one million barrels a day, Mrs T's love affair with the car led her to temporarily abandon her monetarist principles by granting British Leyland a fresh, life-saving injection of public money. In her memoirs she justifies this as a blow against the unions, whose powers she would soon curb: "The company had become a symbol of Britain's industrial decline and of trade union bloody mindedness. However, by the time I entered No.10 it had also begun to symbolize the fightback by management. Michael Edwardes, BL's chairman, had already demonstrated his grit in taking on the trade union militants who had brought the British car industry to its knees."[3]

Her quoting of St Francis of Assisi after her election victory in 1979, "Where there is discord, may we bring harmony" seemed like a bizarre joke, as she went on to wage an unrelenting war that culminated, after a year-long struggle, with the crushing of the miners under their Marxist leader Arthur Scargill.

It was her preoccupation with this fight, and Britain's dire economic problems, that caused Thatcher to put the "great car economy" on hold. She seemingly had no environmental qualms about translating the American scheme of things to a small island like Britain. In fact, during her early years in power, Thatcher displayed no ecological conscience whatsoever. "I find some people thinking of the environment really in quite a kind of airy fairy way as if we could go back to some village life," she pronounced. "Well, some might like it, but it really is quite impossible to do that."[4] And she reacted defensively when Norway and Sweden started to complain about the 'acid rain' phenomenon – pollution from the Sceptr'd Isle falling in precipitation over otherwise pristine Scandinavia, killing life in lakes and harming forests.

However strange it now seems, Thatcher's first administration did preside over some early legislation to curb pollution from cars. In 1981 Tom King, Minister of the Environment, announced that lead in petrol would be reduced to 0.15 grams per litre by 1985. Mike Robinson who has written a study of issues in environmental politics in Britain, says, "This move was not... stimulated by any marked change in the government's attitude to environmental issues; rather, it typified the existing way such issues were handled. Mr King's announcement to the House of Commons was primarily the result of a letter to Whitehall chiefs (later leaked to *The Times*) by the senior medical officer at the Department of Health and Social Security, Sir Henry Yellowlees. In his letter, Yellowlees strongly indicated the risks of atmospheric lead pollution to public health, and urged that the 'simplest and quickest' thing the government should do was to reduce or remove the lead content of petrol. The initial decision to reduce the lead content of petrol and not to introduce lead-free petrol per se was later seized upon by the well-organised pressure group CLEAR

(Campaign for Lead-free Air), established in January 1982. The continued politicisation of the inadequacies of the government's position by CLEAR was aided by the publication of the eighth report of the Royal Commission for Environmental Pollution in April 1983. Within one hour of the report's publication and less than two months away from a General Election, Tom King... promised to seek a European-wide ban on lead in petrol by 1990. The two occasions can be seen as response events and not part of any structured attempt by the political parties voluntarily to bring environmental issues to the fore."[5]

Another reason the "great car economy" got shelved was the coming home to roost of a flock of chickens hatched by Harold Macmillan's 1957-64 Conservative administration. No sooner had Mrs Thatcher gained power, than the motorways Ernest Marples had built began to crack up. Engineers estimated that 100 miles a year would have to be renewed, often with complete rebuilding of road surfaces to a depth of 30 inches. The bill was estimated at £100 million a year, which meant there could be no new road schemes for the time being. An embarrassed Department of Transport tried to gloss over the *débacle* by explaining that motorways built in the 1960s were reaching the end of their "design life". They claimed that the break up of newer sections was a result of increased heavy lorry traffic. Marples was to blame for this too, of course, via his savage emasculation of the rail network. In many cases this could no longer provide a viable alternative for heavy freight traffic, as existed in other, arguably more civilised European countries, such as France and Germany. Kenneth Clarke, then junior transport minister, sadly told the House of Commons, "I do not think that anyone can anticipate a time when the motorway system will be free of major faults."[6]

By August 1980, even Spaghetti Junction, that engineering marvel of yesteryear, was crumbling. This had also been built on the cheap – if £11 million can be called cheap – by bolting together short sections of road. John Coates of the *Sunday Times* reported, "Serious cracks, some nearly an inch wide, have been found in a concrete viaduct." The crack-up of the Spaghetti Junction was a severe embarrassment to the Transport Minister, Norman Fowler, who was already trying to break as gently as possible to the nation news of the huge motorway repair bill. Ron Law, Department of Transport regional controller in the

Midlands, appeared on television to reassure motorists about the "structural integrity" of motorway viaducts in the Birmingham area – just weeks before the cracks in Spaghetti Junction were discovered. When he was asked about this later, Law said he did not feel the cracks jeopardised the structure, a view echoed by Stuart Mustow, who was now West Midlands county surveyor. Shortly afterwards, consulting engineers made a random survey of the beams and were horrified to discover that three quarters of them were in fact in danger of collapsing. An emergency operation was launched to shore up Europe's most complicated motorway interchange.

Alan Whitfield, who was director of the Midlands Roads Construction Unit from 1980-1983, explains, "We threw salt at it in the winter to keep it clear of ice and snow. That salt ran down the joints when the joints failed and spread out over the tops of the joints, over the edges of the beams and the tops of the columns. The visual evidence was overwhelming: spalling, as engineers would call it, which means pieces of concrete falling off, leaving exposed the steel that was meant to be covered and protected by that concrete. Some of the steel deep inside those structures when we exposed it had deteriorated... and you could actually find little pits in the steel that you could put your finger into and you could pull away soft material that had once been steel."[7]

John Coates investigated further. In October 1980, the *Sunday Times* printed his damning verdict: "New faults discovered in the key link in Britain's motorway system indicate shoddy workmanship, the use of under-strength materials and inadequate supervision." According to his investigation, the Spaghetti Junction flaws were merely the tip of an iceberg. "These latest faults occur beneath the massive steel beams that carry the motorway along 13 miles of viaducts," said Coates. "These beams are supported on bearings, which in turn should be securely bedded on cement mortar packed tightly beneath them. But in the case of at least three viaducts – Spaghetti Junction... Witton a little further north and Oldbury on the M5 to the west of the city – engineers have discovered that large quantities of mortar are missing. Some of the bearings rest solely on steel packing plates which were originally put there to bring the beams up to their correct levels. Many of these plates are corroding badly." Tests carried out on behalf of the *Sunday Times* at an independent laboratory showed that even when mortar had been packed in beneath the beams, it was in some cases faulty. It contained too little cement for the required strength and the sand used was sub-standard. "One sample, recovered from underneath a steel beam that dropped dramatically at Spaghetti Junction four months ago, cracking the concrete deck, contained nearly six parts sand to one part cement, instead of the two parts to one specified in the original design," Coates reported. "The quality of the sand used in the mortar was also outside the quality limits specified because it contained too many fine particles. These can weaken the mortar unless extra cement is added." Another sample from the same viaduct contained even more sand: 6.3 parts to one of cement. The laboratory test report said: "We have found evidence of a serious deficiency in cement, the use of an excessively fine sand and poor workmanship in packing and compacting the mortar."

Bernard Clark, a structural engineer who had been an expert witness in major lawsuits involving construction failures, told Coates: "This is an engineering mortar of the quality normally used for brick walls that carry little more than their own weight."

The sand-cement ratio of a sample taken from Oldbury Viaduct was 3.7:1. The sand also contained too many fine particles. A sample from the Witton Viaduct on the M6 was all cement. "The problem here is that neat cement is weak because it shrinks when it sets," Coates explained.

"The consulting engineers for the whole of the Midland Links project were Sir Owen Williams and Partners, who designed and supervised the construction. Arthur Price, their partner in charge of the scheme, says tests were carried out to ensure that the mortar specified in the design was strong enough. But because the road was built so quickly, he doubted that samples were taken during construction to ensure that the mortar came up to the specified strength."

When Coates asked if the workmanship was inspected, Price replied: "There would not have been 100 per cent quality control. The staff was not available. There would have been spot checks only, when the site engineers could get access."

Cameron Johnstone, director of RM Douglas, who built

Witton Viaduct, said: "The cement we used was strength-tested during installation of the mortar. I have been told that the standard of workmanship on this contract was good."

Maurice Couchman, chairman of A Monk & Co, who built Spaghetti Junction, said: "All the work was inspected as it went along in the normal way. Twelve months after the job was handed over, an inspection was carried out by our client." A row now developed when it was revealed that Monk had been invited to tender for repairs to 3,400 metal bearings. Had it won the contract, the company would have been paid taxpayers' money to put right faults for which it was itself responsible. A Transport Department spokesman who was asked why Monk had been invited to tender, replied: "Monk are on our approved list for this type of work. They have carried out many contracts for the department, covering a wide variety of road and bridge works and their work has generally been satisfactory."

John Tyme summed up the situation in a soundbite from the 1990s: "The whole road programme has been built on one gigantic spoof. Billion upon billion upon billion pounds has been spent over 40 years and where are we? Gridlock!"[8]

The beleaguered road construction industry was forced to seize any opportunity to bolster its sagging reputation. When two swans were discovered to be nesting in the middle of the route of the £2.4 million Beccles by-pass in Suffolk, work was halted on the particular section until all seven eggs had hatched and the swans had moved on. Badgers were rather slower on the uptake. It took four years before they began using special tunnels made for them under the M5 in Somerset, and as they did so at night there were fewer photo opportunities.

Throughout the 1980s, half a million new cars came onto the roads of Britain each year. As the economy grew stronger, Thatcher began once more to talk of creating "the great car economy". And as she gave her blessing to the car, so the Iron Lady carried forward a Conservative tradition of distrust for the iron rail – she had a deep rooted dislike of train travel. Sir Alastair Morton, who at the time of writing is head of the Strategic Rail Authority, recalls, "I know two senior civil servants who were present at meetings with Margaret Thatcher, which she physically terminated by getting up and leaving when the words 'integrated transport plan' were mentioned. To her it sounded Marxist. Nutty!"[9] The Labour-controlled Greater London Council's 'Fares fair' scheme – which slashed Underground fares to encourage more people to use public transport – also greatly irked Thatcher because it ran counter to her monetarist beliefs. Roger Higman, senior transport campaigner for Friends of the Earth, says, "Mrs Thatcher abolished the GLC for many reasons but one of them was Fares Fair. She hated it."[10]

In 1986, at the opening of the final section of the £980 million M25, Thatcher lauded it as one of the world's greatest highways. (The London orbital motorway was the successor to the failed London motorway box of ring roads.) She attacked those who had criticised this "magnificent British achievement" that had taken 14 years to build. The PM cut a ribbon and helped to remove a line of traffic cones. A minute after traffic was allowed through, a car broke down but was quickly removed by police before a hold-up could develop. The opening of the new section brought the interchange between the M25 and the M1 into full use, handling more than 150,000 vehicles a day. The Department of the Environment proudly claimed that the new section cost £4 million a kilometre to build because of special measures to protect the environment, including the planting of more than 2.1 million trees.

The government White Paper, *Policy for Roads*, spelled out the idea of the M25; a motorway built almost entirely through land officially declared as Green Belt. It stated that it would "provide a quick, safe and convenient route round Greater London; it will complete motorway links between Heathrow, Gatwick and Stansted (airports); it will act as a general distributor enabling drivers to find their way in and out of London by the most convenient route; and it will take heavy through traffic away from communities on the outskirts of London and help to relieve some routes through the centres". The reality was that it very rapidly became a motoring nightmare, attracting huge volumes of traffic, and becoming popularly known as "the biggest traffic jam in Europe".

Before this happened, the M25 enjoyed a brief honeymoon with motorists. A clandestine "M25 Club" was said to exist, with one member completing the 117-mile 'circuit' in 68 minutes, clocking up an average speed of 103 mph.

More spectacularly, a man once drove along it for 20 miles

with two burst rear tyres, wearing down his wheel rims until his petrol tank was dragging on the road in a shower of sparks. Amazingly, he survived. There was also the old lady who decided one day – in best British eccentric tradition – to go for a bike ride in the fast lane during rush-hour. She also lived to tell the tale. More seriously, less than a year after it had been opened, a lorry carrying chemical detergents caught fire, east of London Colney in Hertfordshire, burning so fiercely that the police were unable to control it. This caused an eight-mile traffic tailback and destroyed part of the surface of the road – a precursor of hundreds more accidents, a great many of which were fatal.

After the opening of the final section of the road by Thatcher, Michael Watkins of the *The Times* visited Godstone, Surrey, just off the motorway. He found that while, if it were put to the vote, there might be an almost unanimous vote in favour of the M25, none of the villagers actually wanted to use it. Retired councillor Arthur Dumville, told Watkins that before the M25, "Godstone had become a no-go area". You could "die and decompose" on the pavement before traffic would allow you to cross the road. Watkins said: "In this respect, then the M25 was a godsend. Congested traffic from the A25 and the A22 found speedy relief on the brave new orbital, leaving Godstone to enjoy the somnolence of gentler times." At least that was the theory. The reality, according to Dumville, was that restraints on traffic ceased to apply; allowing local sand quarry lorries access to the M25 through the village and attracting motorists returning to A roads to escape from 'Motorway Madness'.

Moira Younger, part-owner of Godstone Village Stores, said: "When there's an accident on the M25, road repairs or a jam – and it's not exactly a unique occurrence – all the traffic comes back through the village. Even so, I've heard no one say it hurts Godstone. Business hasn't suffered. I'm unreservedly in favour of the M25, although I'm frightened to use it myself. It's like an arena. I feel forced to drive faster than I want to."

Peter Gottelier, a local estate agent, said the M25 had been great for business. "Suddenly Godstone was nearer London-Heathrow-Gatwick, but also offered a taste of country life." He claimed that yuppies were taking out mortgages of £140,000 and more. "It's terrific for business. I keep telling myself we've reached the ceiling, but that ceiling keeps being raised.

"I avoid the M25 myself, pure funk. There's a major smash about once a fortnight. Homework on the pressure of traffic was appallingly done." Watkins said memories of a 26 car pile-up in 1984, when the motorway was partially completed, were still fresh in the villagers' minds. Nine people died and 13 were injured. At the Godstone police motorway centre, Sergeant Harry Sale said, "The M25 was designed to accommodate a certain volume of traffic, but we're beyond the 1990 forecast already." A spokesman for the local sand quarry, ruminated on the problem and came up with a novel solution. "What that orbital needs is another orbital to orbit the orbital," he said.

By 1994 the M25 was very much a mixed blessing for the towns along its route. Don Conaghan reported for the *Daily Telegraph*: "For the 22,000 people who live in Reigate, congestion in the town centre and along the approaches to the M25 nearby has become a daily ordeal of traffic queues, noise and exhaust pollution. During rush hours, the High Street of the Surrey town is choked with cars, articulated lorries and trucks from local quarries." Lessons had obviously been learned. Conaghan reported: "Rather than building roads to ease the flow on existing ones, the local authority hopes to improve public transport, persuade commuters to leave cars at home, and possibly take through traffic north of the town. In the past, new roads in the area have attracted more drivers. This trend has led to almost continuous traffic to and from the M23 and M25. On the M25, Junction 8 at Reigate has become one of the worst for traffic hold-ups. Mr David Neal, chairman of Reigate Traders' Guild and the owner of a gift shop in Church Street, described the M25 as 'a mixed blessing'. 'We all hoped that it would ease pressure on the A25, which is notoriously congested here,' he said. 'For a short period after the motorway opened, things improved. But all that changed when people realised the M25 was all connected up. Reigate has become a "feeder" town for the M25. The traffic is beginning to deter some shoppers and, frankly, I don't think the town can take much more.'" Lady Thomas, chair of Surrey County Council's transport committee, said: "We can't keep providing road space. We are trying to persuade people to move from cars and take to their feet, bicycles or other modes of transport."

As the M25 was getting into its awesome, horrific swing, politicians were experiencing the first glimmerings of awareness that there might be growing concern for the environment among electors to both right and left of traditional political divides. In 1988 Thatcher made her famous speech to the Royal Society in which, for the first time, she appeared to have developed an ecological conscience. In tones carefully modified by a speech therapist laid on by Saatchi and Saatchi, the suddenly Green Lady said: "For generations, we have assumed that the efforts of mankind would leave the fundamental equilibrium of the world's systems and atmosphere stable. But it is possible that with all these enormous changes (population, agriculture, use of fossil fuels) concentrated into such a short period of time, we have unwittingly begun a massive experiment with the system of this planet itself... In studying the system of the earth and its atmosphere we have no laboratory in which to carry out controlled experiments. We have to rely on observations of natural systems. We need to identify particular areas of research which will help to establish cause and effect. We need to consider in more detail the likely effects of change within precise timescales. And to consider the wider implications for policy – for energy production, for fuel efficiency, for reforestation... We must ensure that what we do is founded on good science to establish cause and effect."

Mike Robinson is generous in assessing Thatcher's 'conversion' to the Green cause. He says her Royal Society speech, along with follow-up pronouncements to the Conservative party conference a month later, were valuable in breaking quiescence in UK environmental politics. "These largely unexpected announcements meant that the environment was led rapidly back into a political ascendancy, and thus began a late mid-term phase of environmental interest. This renewed interest was exhibited in four main ways. Firstly Mrs Thatcher displayed an apparent willingness continually to speak out for an area of policy which she had previously shown little interest in. Secondly, the Environmental Protection Bill was introduced, which was intended to provide a comprehensive framework to address a range of matters including waste disposal, pollution control and nature conservation. Thirdly, the government White Paper *This Common Inheritance* was published, which is the most comprehensive attempt yet to develop a national environmental policy. Fourthly, both the Labour Party and the Liberal Democrats produced major environmental policy documents in the wake of the White Paper respectively entitled *An Earthly Chance and What Price our Planet?*"[12]

The following year, when her government launched its *Roads for Prosperity* White Paper – a £12 billion inter-urban road expansion programme to be implemented in the next 10 years – it was given environmental 'spin'. It contained plans to build 230 miles of new motorway and widen 500 miles of existing motorway. It would transform sections of a number of key routes, such as the M1 between London and Leeds, the M25 and the M6 from Leicestershire to the Scottish border, into eight lane mega-highways. It was argued that by-passes would help to conserve villages, and there were promises that trees would be planted alongside all new motorways. This worried the Institute of Road Transport Engineers. An article in *Transport Engineer*, their in-house journal, acknowledged that planting a tree for every vehicle put on the road "should be a help in neutralizing the emissions of carbon dioxide being blamed for the warming of the earth's atmosphere". But it also pointed out, "There is hardly a collision more violent than a vehicle hitting a tree." The article said that while "the leafy lanes of Britain may be a treasure to uplift the heart... to apply the sentiment to trunk roads carrying fast-moving traffic is thoughtless, if not irresponsible."

The comedian Spike Milligan wrote an article for *The Times* in March 1990 in which he imagined himself to be Cecil Parkinson, Thatcher's current Minister of Transport, planning *Roads for Prosperity*. The first thing Milligan's incarnation as Parkinson calls for is a map showing conservation areas, sites of special scientific interest and areas of outstanding natural beauty. "There were acres of it!," he exclaims euphorically. "Now there are those who are violently opposed to my plans. Take Friends of the Earth. Fiends of the Earth, I call them; they all have motor cars. How do they expect to get from A to B without suitable roads? You can't drive over ploughed fields, but you can if you build a road through them. And I'm going to have grass, yes, grass, each side of the motorway, and before long, if you drive slowly, you'll see daisies and dandelions... Will it not be a pleasant sight seeing British-made Rolls-Royces and Bentleys (which people can now afford under a Tory government) passing down my grass-verged motorways? It can only encourage the poor to become richer... Roads are the answer; roads, roads and more roads."[12]

Milligan's assessment was remarkably accurate. However, one place where "roads, roads and more roads" was not the answer was London – too many Tory votes were at stake. Thousands of homes in the capital were threatened by a revamp of the Motorway Box idea called the 'London Assessment Studies'. To ease congestion in the inner city the Department of Transport had come up with a series of options that included proposals for miles of dual carriageways to the south, west and east of the capital. New trunk roads were planned from Croydon to Lewisham, Catford to Wandsworth, and Highgate to King's Cross. Up to 8,000 homes would have to be demolished and approximately 30,000 would be permanently affected. Peter Walker, who had successfully fought the Motorway Box 20 years previously, found to his horror that the £100,000 flat he had bought in Battersea Rise was threatened by a new urban clearway. Walker, who organised LAMM (Londoners Against Motorway Madness) to fight the Studies, said, "There are people in the Department of Transport who are hypnotised by the gleam of the hub cap. Londoners do not want new roads. They are unnecessary, damaging and expensive." ALARM (All London Against the Road Menace) organised a capital-wide campaign. As a result of uncertainty caused by the scheme, a property blight settled over the city; quite out of keeping with Thatcherite ideals. Roger Higman, of Friends of the Earth, says, "Suddenly you had a population in London who realised there was too much traffic on the roads and that road building only encouraged more traffic, which creates more pollution. They said, 'Our houses are going to be demolished, our children are being poisoned, our local council which was pursuing sensible transport policies has been abolished. And we're not happy about this.' There were protests and marches. It was all on the street and in the public eye."[13] The uproar so rattled the government that in the spring of 1990, Parkinson announced that the Studies would be scrapped. At the same time the Archway Road scheme opposed by John Tyme was also finally and quietly disposed of. Instead of new roads, there would be £250 million worth of improvements at a number of junctions, resulting in the loss of 'only' 200 houses. Close attention would be given to provision for pedestrians and cyclists, said Parkinson. Significantly, his climb-down came just before local council elections.

Thatcher was ousted as prime minister in November 1990, after losing a leadership election by just four votes to the pro-European Michael Heseltine. As the axe fell and she was replaced, not by the hated Heseltine at all but by her Chancellor, John Major, Thatcher uttered one of the wisest pronouncements of her long career. "It's a funny old world," she said – and sailed into a stately sunset as a baroness.

It is indeed a funny old world. It was all the rage in the Thatcher years to blame the social chaos of the modern era – rising crime, drug abuse, divorce and abortion – on the so-called permissive 1960s. Yet, as author Ian MacDonald has so succinctly pointed out, such chaos "was created neither by the hippies (who wanted us all to be together) nor by the New Left radicals, all of whom were socialists of some description. So far as anything in the Sixties can be blamed for the demise of the compound entity of society, it was the natural desire of the 'masses' to lead easier, pleasanter lives, own their own homes, follow their own fancies and move out of the communal collective. What mass society unconsciously began in the Sixties, Thatcher and Reagan raised to the level of ideology in the Eighties: the materialistic individualisation – and total fragmentation – of Western Society."[14] Bearing in mind the Iron Lady's thoughts on society (she once famously said there was no such thing), MacDonald has a point.

The car was a tenet of Thatcherism. Steven Norris, former Conservative Parliamentary Under Secretary for Roads, says, "It is well known that Mrs Thatcher was a great devotee of what she called 'the great car economy'. But I think she was also expressing the view that said, 'Look, car ownership is a symbol of individual success,' – that was very much an element of Mrs Thatcher's policy – [and] 'it is a symbol of individual freedom' – very much a Conservative principle."[15] But while the Conservatives were pro-car, at this stage of the game neither of the other parties were exactly anti-car. A dangerous vacuum had developed. The campaign against new roads was apolitical. Three key campaigners – John Stewart, Jonathan Bray and Emma Must – display scant faith in the political process in general as they look back on Thatcher's time in power. "[The] concerned middle-classes could not turn to either of the other two main parties for any real assistance for, while both Labour and the Liberal Democrats favoured better public transport, in the mid 1980s neither was clearly articulating opposition to unwanted development. It was perhaps logical then, that Middle England became part of a protest movement that operated outside established political structures.

"Equally excluded from establishment politics were the growing number of people who were dismayed at what they perceived as the national – and indeed global – destruction of the natural environment. Their 'deep green' concerns were not taken on board by the major political parties; and certainly not by the groupings on the far left that had attracted many radicals of earlier generations. The relatively unstructured 'anti-roads' movement that was emerging in the mid-1980s was to become, a few years later, a natural vehicle of protest for the green children of Thatcher."[16]

Battle was about to be joined.

7

THE CRUELLEST CUT

John Major, who succeeded Margaret Thatcher as prime minister, found himself in a no win situation. He had to defend his predecessor's record yet at the same time show that his would be a more caring Conservatism, of the sort Mrs T had derisively dismissed as 'wet'. Derided in the Press as a 'grey' man, Major was desperate to prove that he was in fact his 'own man'. Unfortunately, he seemed unable to establish any solid independent ground between the Tory political polarities. Instead, finding himself standing on quicksand, he floundered – bending first in one direction, then the other. On the few occasions Major did take a stand, he invariably got it wrong. Twyford Down was a case in point. It is a savage irony that it was the government of John Major – the would-be good guy; a citizens' charter, cricket-loving sort of chap – that was ultimately responsible for one of the most wanton acts of environmental vandalism ever perpetrated in Britain.

Twyford Down was a magnificent chalk downland ridge that provided a backdrop to Winchester, the cathedral city that had for centuries been the capital of England – it was only in the reign of Henry III (1216-72) that London displaced it. The history of the Down itself stretched back to the dawn of history. It was inhabited in the Bronze Age by men who grew crops on high ground, finding this simpler than draining the valleys. By the Iron Age, settlement was concentrated around a fertile clay 'cap' at the Down's apex. Tracks led down to the valley, from where fresh water had to be carried each day from the River Itchen. In the Middle Ages, herds were grazed on Twyford Down and it became criss-crossed with trackways, or drover's paths, some of which by the modern age were up to 20 feet deep, having been eroded over hundreds of years. Sometime in the 1800s these had been inaccurately named "Dongas" by someone at Winchester College with colonial connections – it is a Matabele word meaning "drainage channels".

By the late 20th century, Twyford Down had been officially designated as an Area of Outstanding Natural Beauty with two sites on it declared to be of special scientific interest. For citizens of Winchester, in the words of Professor Martin Biddle, a local archaeologist, the Down was "perhaps unique in providing a thriving modern city with a visual perspective reaching deep into its remote past. Here it was possible in the course of an hour or so to walk from the twentieth century to the prehistoric past, or even glance from one to another in the course of a moment at work or in school."[1]

Today that perspective is no more. An ugly gash 400 feet wide, 100 feet deep and nearly a mile long has ripped the Down apart. It houses part of the M3 motorway – the Down has been sliced in two to save a few minutes on the journey from London to Southampton.

The cutting of Twyford Down was opposed in the beginning by true blue Tories. In his history of Friends of the Earth, Robert Lamb writes, "By no stretch of the imagination could the local protesters be dismissed as leftist rabble-rousers. On the whole they were prosperous and solidly middle-class townspeople, so dominated by inveterate Tory voters that it was sometimes said in jest that the Conservative vote in Winchester had to be weighed, not counted."[2]

They were led by Barbara Bryant, a mother of three and a Conservative councillor on Winchester City Council, who describes herself as "at home in the free market". At the time of writing, she is chief executive of North Hampshire Chamber of Commerce. Bryant, originally from East Sussex, moved to Winchester from London in 1978 with her husband Dudley, a chartered surveyor. She lived in Twyford village and would walk Trooper, her Labrador dog on the Down. "I loved it, there was something so special about the way it had not been touched, I mean farmed or ploughed for more than 2,000 years. I would walk along the dongas and look at the butterflies sunning themselves on the slopes while Trooper went chasing after rabbits. I've always loved that short downland turf."[3]

The original plans for the M3 had involved the creation of a 10 lane highway across the Winchester Water Meadows. When this was thwarted by John Tyme back in the mid 1970s, various other routes were put forward by the Department of Transport before it settled on cutting the Down. Bryant recalls, "The local greengrocer – you know, one of these people who knows everything that's going on – said to me, 'Here, have you heard the latest? They're going to put a motorway through the Down.' Well, I just laughed and thought, 'Old Fred's really got it wrong this time.' Unfortunately, of course, he was absolutely right.[4]

"The thing was Winchester College owned the Down and wanted at all costs to keep the road away from their beloved Water Meadows – you couldn't blame them for that. The great irony was that the Down had been bought in the 1920s by two masters at the College to save it from development – there were plans then to build houses on it. Anyway, the two masters eventually handed the Down over to the college for safekeeping."

As protests against the motorway gathered force, the college would frequently be accused of acting irresponsibly in selling the Down to the Department of Transport (for a reported £300,000).[5] Its reply was that all the other routes considered would have caused more harm but Bryant points out, "This is a multi-faceted story. What has never been properly explained is why the road **had** to go to the east of Winchester. Why not to the west? A much more logical choice – but a large tract of the land in that direction was owned by Lord Louis Mountbatten." Mountbatten, a great grandson of Queen Victoria, supreme commander of Allied troops in South East Asia during World War Two, and former Viceroy of India was assassinated by the IRA in 1979. Bryant thinks he used his considerable influence to block all plans that would route the motorway west of Winchester, close to his estates at Broadlands, near Romsey. She said informants in Whitehall had spoken of a Cabinet minute stating that Lord Mountbatten should be kept informed of all developments concerning trunk road development around Winchester.[6]

A public inquiry into the Twyford Down proposal got underway in 1985. Opponents of the route – gathering at first under the banner of the M3 Joint Action group, and led by Bryant and fellow Conservative councillor David Croker –

suggested the far more environmentally friendly, but also costly alternative of tunnelling through the Down. This was rejected, "with some reluctance", by Dudley Leaker, the inspector. His report said, "Because of its high extra cost it presumably could only be carried out at the expense or deferment of worthwhile projects elsewhere in the country. But this proposal also deals in intangible values and the preservation of our heritage... so it is with some reluctance that I have to conclude that I cannot recommend (it) in spite of its superiority in respecting sensitive areas of environmental and historic importance."

But growing support for a tunnel forced a reopening of the inquiry in 1987. Bryant says of Leaker, "we believed that his report recognised the potential benefits of a tunnel and, heartened by these findings, we believed, somewhat naïvely, that free to present all the evidence of the environmental damage to the reopened inquiry we would achieve a different route for the M3. By that time we had a substantial group of local and national organisations and individuals supporting our objections."[7] These included the World Wide Fund for Nature, all the major English archaeological societies, environmentalists such as the wildlife artist David Shepherd, and the scientist Miriam Rothschild.

Bryant had put her faith in the inherent justice of British institutions, but this took a severe knock when she learned that Leaker had again been appointed as inspector at the reopened inquiry, despite an official guideline which states, "If the reopened Inquiry is to deal with a matter on which the Inspector, who held the original Inquiry, has already expressed an opinion, a different Inspector will probably be appointed to hold it." Winchester Council wrote to the Lord Chancellor's Department asking why Leaker had been appointed. The less-than-convincing reply was: "Mr Leaker had an advantage that no other person can have in that he will have heard all the evidence at the Inquiries."

At this point a note of farce was introduced with the announcement that Mr Leaker had fallen and broken a leg while out hill-walking, and the inquiry would have to be postponed. Shortly afterwards an official at the Department of Transport wrote to all objectors saying, "Mr Leaker has had to withdraw from the inquiry, and a further Inspector has now been nominated to sit in his place."

During a three month delay, before the inquiry reopened with Air Vice Marshall Maughan as inspector, Winchester City Council withdrew its backing for the cutting of Twyford Down and gave its support for a tunnel. Hampshire County Council, on the other hand, came out against the tunnel. The *Hampshire Chronicle* said: "The decision was taken behind closed doors... Members voted to exclude the press and public from the debate despite the fact that the meeting is normally open to the public." Such divisions harmed the objectors' case.

But environmental 'heavyweights' were united in opposing the cut. Dr Geoffrey Wainwright, principal inspector of English Heritage, responsible for archaeology and ancient monuments, told the inquiry, "Our conclusion remains that this route will cause the maximum archaeological damage." David Coleman, regional officer for the Countryside Commission, said, "The route will be an eyesore in this landscape. Breaching the Downs with an enormous man-made canyon so close to the natural route of the River Itchen would be entirely against the grain of the landscape." Winchester College, while still supporting the cutting of Twyford Down, magnanimously said it had no objection to a tunnel alternative.

Maughan reported that the tunnel idea "attracted the highest degree of perceptible public support of any route." However, it was agreed by both its supporters and Department of Transport experts, that it could cost in the region of £85-£95 million and take four or five years to construct. The result was that Maughan rejected the tunnel and opted for the cutting of the Down.

The inquiry made headlines locally, but failed to attract national media coverage. Barbara Bryant, determined to make Twyford a national issue and "shame the Government into saving the Down", was confirmed in her resolve by Margaret Thatcher's 1988 speech to the Royal Society. "Environment shot up the political agenda," said Bryant. "For the first time within the Conservative Party it was acceptable to express concern for the environment. Before that you were thought to be slightly lunatic."[8]

The Joint Action Group invited Jonathon Porritt, Eton-educated director of Friends of the Earth and member of Prince Charles' unofficial 'kitchen cabinet' of advisers, to speak at a public meeting in Winchester. *The Times* ran a story by Michael McCarthy, its environment correspondent, headlined "£53m Road Schemes Put Government's Green Policy On Test", drawing attention to the threat to Twyford Down. The *Daily Telegraph* carried a picture reconstruction of the proposed cut through the Down and reported, "In what is likely to be one of the most controversial planning decisions of the decade, an inquiry inspector has recommended that permission be given to build an extension of the M3 through one of the most heavily protected landscapes in the country." Bryant was jubilant, declaring, "After four years the campaign to save Twyford Down had finally achieved national prominence."[9]

There were drawbacks to this. At one point Bryant found herself under surveillance by MI5. A friend – "a level-headed lady not given to dramatics" – who had once worked for the security services telephoned her from abroad and said that from what she had heard on the line she was positive that Bryant's phone was being tapped. In another incident the line went dead for several minutes, followed by a call saying, "Good afternoon, this is the telephone engineers. You have just reported a fault – no dialling tone on your line. It seems to be all right now." Bryant was baffled. "I had not reported the fault – I couldn't. No one else knew there was a problem, which anyway had only lasted a few minutes. From that time on the family accepted that our phone was tapped."[10]

In November 1989, during Prime Minister's Question Time in the House of Commons, John Browne, MP for Winchester, asked Thatcher if she could "assure the House that the Secretary of State for Transport will speedily be given sufficient funds to ensure that whatever route is finally selected, it will be friendly to the special and historic environment around Winchester, which is a national asset?" Thatcher replied, "The Secretaries of State for Transport and Environment are currently considering the Inspectors' Reports. I cannot anticipate what their decisions will be, but I know they fully understand the importance of environmental issues in cases such as this."[11]

On February 20 1990, a few months after Thatcher had been ousted as leader, Cecil Parkinson, Secretary of State for Transport, published his roads programme. It contained an appendix in which tenders were announced for a 3.7 mile section of the M3 that included the cut through Twyford Down. Sir Derek Barber, chairman of the Countryside Commission, said he was "just flabbergasted."

Parkinson made the official announcement a week later. He said the decision came after extensive consultations with local authorities, interested bodies, and the public. He said although he had initially been attracted to the idea of a tunnel, "the advantages of a tunnel scheme did not outweigh the substantial additional cost and the extensive delay in completing the M3." The cutting was estimated to cost £37 million and involve the removal of some 300,000 tons of rock and spoil. The tunnel scheme would have cost £92 million and entailed removing approximately 1,740,000 cubic metres of spoil.

In a leading article headlined "Motorway Madness", *The Times* said Parkinson had made the wrong decision. It said the cutting of Twyford Down "is as extreme and irreversible an act of environmental spoiling as can be imagined." It continued: "The conclusion must be that the Government's stated commitment to the preservation of the natural environment can in principle always be over-trumped by the need for an improved transport infrastructure and considerations of finance. The economy, and not the environment, is the greater imperative..." The article referred to the cutting of Twyford Down as "a vast and hideous excavation running through its centre, totally destroying its character as an outstanding treasure of natural landscape".

The protesters had six weeks to appeal. They set up the Twyford Down Association, whose aim was to seek support from the rest of the country; arguing that if a site such as Twyford Down could be sacrificed to road-building, nowhere else in Britain was safe. Robert Lamb says, "Its founding members could be stereotyped as traditional upholders of 'Middle England' values." The president of the Association was Professor Martin Biddle and members included Jonathon Porritt, Miriam Rothschild and Maldwin Drummond, a deputy lieutenant of Hampshire and a Countryside Commissioner. Old boys of Winchester College were persuaded to campaign against the destruction of the Down. Bryant reported breathlessly, "They contributed about £25,000, but they also wrote letters – very erudite letters, from impressive addresses – to the DoT and to ministers – often on first-name terms."[12]

Bryant and David Croker campaigned against Parkinson's decision at the Conservative Party conference. Following this, they unsuccessfully filed a motion to the Queen's Bench Division of the High Court to stop the routing of the motorway through the Down. Here they met other anti-motorway protesters who suggested that they take the fight to the European Commission, on the grounds that British highway procedure contravened European legislation by failing to carry out prior environmental impact assessments. In retrospect this was a great mistake. Carlo Ripa di Meana, the European Environment Commissioner, infuriated Major's government by calling on it to halt seven motorway schemes, including Twyford Down. Jonathon Porritt later expressed regrets at taking the Brussels option, "Perhaps we should have foreseen that the more explicitly interventionist di Meana became, the more firmly Twyford Down's fate was sealed. It wasn't just a question of the usual loss of face involved in a Government having to change its mind, but of national pride." He continues ironically, "Better by far to assert our inalienable sovereignty by destroying one of the most important conservation and archaeological sites in the country than to be forced to recant by a bunch of meddling Euro-Federalists."[13]

Peter Kunzlik, Professor of European Business Law at the Nottingham Law School, who advised the protesters on European law, says: "An additional irritant was the fact that Mr Major, then newly appointed as Prime Minister, was away from home attending the Commonwealth Conference in Harare, Zimbabwe, when the news broke. Thus, at his first Commonwealth Conference as Prime Minister, he found himself having to defend his Government's environmental policy to press and media journalists rather than being able to project his own political agenda."[14]

Bryant says, "Gus O'Donnell, Major's press secretary, who has close contacts with Winchester told us that Major just exploded. I think that from then on he just dug his heels in and refused to budge. I honestly think that had Mrs Thatcher still been in power we could have saved the Down. She had a bit more about her as a leader, and we had channels to her."[15]

Meanwhile, Prince Charles – doubtless influenced by Porritt – helped the Green cause in general but received hostile reactions from Major's government when he told a meeting of the Royal

Society for Nature Conservation, "We can go on nibbling away at the corners of our remaining unspoilt and valuable habitats, justifying our actions on the basis of economic necessity, or even personal convenience, but what will the overall picture be like... in 50 years' time?" He then quoted government statistics: 687 sites of Special Scientific Interest, 14 percent of the total, had been lost or damaged between 1984 and 1988. He also cited a study by the Wildlife Trust showing that road building plans for the South East would destroy or damage 372 sites of Special Scientific Interest in the next decade. The Prince later described the European Commission's powers to assess environmental impact as an "important building block for the future". He said, "I think it is important to recognise that in many areas of environment policy the European Community as the only body in the world with a supranational authority to legislate to protect the environment, is ahead of the world." With Major still furious over di Meana's intervention on Twyford Down and other British motorway plans, the Foreign Office vetoed a visit Charles had been due to make to the Commission's Environment Section in Brussels.

In 1991, in an attempt to placate Major and allow him to save face, the protesters suggested a toll tunnel through the Down with part of the profits used to fund conservation work – a free market solution calculated to appeal to a Conservative administration. But Major was still in no mood to compromise and when John Browne tabled a formal Parliamentary question to the Secretary of State for Transport on whether he would adopt the plan for a toll tunnel, the answer was blunt and to the point: "No. We have no intention of reopening the... decision... on this much-needed scheme which followed twenty years of debate and four (sic) public inquiries." A key group of protesters then met Malcolm Rifkind who had succeeded Parkinson as Secretary of State for Transport to try to persuade him of the viability of its proposal. At his suggestion, they prepared a feasibility study which showed that if a toll of £1 were charged per vehicle, the tunnel would break even in 15 years. It was all to no avail. Two days before Christmas 1991, the Transport Department announced that a contract for preliminary work on the cutting of Twyford Down had been awarded to the John Mowlem construction firm.

In January 1992, the start of construction work was greeted by protests from local residents. From this moment on the face of the Twyford Down protest changed, growing progressively more militant. Bryant stuck with Porrit and Friends of the Earth, arranging the occupation of one of two small farm-track bridges over a railway line, due to be demolished by Mowlem as part of further preparatory work. She recalls, "The carefully organised and disciplined protest was to involve a small group of FoE campaigners. The intention was to remain on the bridge until legally required to move. It was a bright February day and the occupiers were brought coffee and sandwiches by the locals. The work was due to start at midnight on the Saturday, and by late afternoon the police arrived. The FoE campaign leader, Roger Higman, and I, for the Twyford Down Association, were informed by the police that they had powers to ask us to leave the site, and were now doing just that. Within a few minutes, our supporters had all vacated the site."[16]

However, unknown to Bryant, her fellow-campaigner David Croker had come to the conclusion that a more militant stance was now unavoidable. "(If direct action) is the only thing we can do, then we must do it," said Croker. "It's the logical conclusion to the fight."[17] He made contact with the militant ecological movement Earth First! His action greatly upped the ante in the battle for Twyford Down, and though he did not fully realise it at the time, Croker was playing with fire.

Earth First! had been set up in the United States in 1980 as a reaction to ineffectual 'mainstream' ecological groups by people perhaps best described in British English as "well dodgy". The organisation, or "disorganisation" as it liked to think of itself, relied for its inspiration on Edward Abbey's novel *The Monkey Wrench Gang*. *Abbey*, born in the town of Indiana, Pennsylvania in 1927, later developed a fierce love for the American West. He said, "I fell in love with the country, the land so deeply that I've been offended ever since by what some people want to do with it." Before he died in Tucson, Arizona in 1989, Abbey had written a considerable body of literature in praise of the American wilderness that also vehemently attacked industrial consumerism. 'The Monkey Wrench Gang' of his best known work are four anarchists dedicated to halting the incursions of civilisation into wilderness areas. They knock down advertising billboards, blow up bridges, strip mines, drilling rigs and logging machines, *and sabotage new roads.* One line of dialogue from the novel was particularly applicable to Twyford Down – "We're up against a mad machine... which mangles mountains and devours men," says one of the gang, "Somebody has to try and stop it."[18]

A devotee of Abbey's work, Dave Foreman, one of the co-founders of Earth First! similarly exhorted his followers to sabotage modern technology that threatened the environment. Foreman told his followers, "If you aren't a warrior I suggest you find another group. It's time for a warrior society to rise up out of the earth and put ourselves in front of the juggernaut of destruction."[19] *Ecodefense*, a manual produced by Foreman, contained hints on how to attack offices of companies guilty of pollution. The FBI investigated Earth First! and in 1991 after a 30 month undercover operation, four activists were imprisoned for conspiracy and destruction of property – trying to sabotage the water supply to the city of Phoenix, Arizona. Foreman himself was arrested at gunpoint in an FBI raid, and another Earth First! leader blown up in a mysterious bomb attack.

An early move to establish Earth First! in Britain in 1987 by former Greenpeace worker Chris Laughton failed, but in 1991 two further education students, Jake Burbridge and Jason Torrance, from Hastings, in East Sussex, managed to set up a more enduring network. Derek Wall, a British Green activist, who has made a study of the movement, describes a meeting he had with an anonymous Earth First! member later that year. "We drove around the Bristol streets, as a security precaution... As the rain beat down, he told me that his Earth First! cell had been anonymously sabotaging JCBs and other items of heavy plant in the West Country... At one point he opened a briefcase full of xeroxed copies of *Ecodefense*."[20]

One of the Earth First! activists with whom David Croker made contact was Davy Garland, an ex-Green Party, ex-Communist Party member, "deeply attached to working-class community politics... Garland is notorious for his advocacy of strident militancy and had briefly been held by the police for selling the militant newsletter Terraist, a pun on the Latin term for 'earth'."[21] Garland describes the meeting thus: "He turned up in his little sporty car and we were talking about making a camp (and) defences. David Croker was offering a kind of old army base... The rail bridges were coming up so we were going to have that as a major action."[22]

In a scene reminiscent of an Ealing comedy, as Bryant and the thoroughly respectable, middle-class Friends of the Earth campaigners left the bridge, Croker and other members of the Twyford Down Association set up a diversion that distracted the police. Dreadlocked Earth First! activists moved through the undergrowth to chain themselves to Mowlem's machinery. There were six arrests.

Word now spread that an anti-road camp along the lines of the so-called 'peace camps' at Greenham Common was going to be set up at Twyford. Attracted by the idea, more and more Earth First! activists and other radicals began arriving at Twyford Down. One of them was Alex Begg, who said, "I thought this was a great idea, but being as I was like somebody living in a house, I wasn't going to do anything about it myself. But when I heard somebody was setting up an anti-road camp at Twyford I was very excited." Jason Torrance said the radicals were initially discouraged by Roger Higman, of Friends of the Earth, who told them, "No, no. Silly idea. You know the last thing we want is loads of people trampling on an SSSI (site of special scientific interest)."[23]

However, shortly afterwards, Friends of the Earth took on the idea and set up their own camp. Barbara Bryant, studiously ignoring the Earth First! protesters recalls, "A brave band of FoE campaigners pitched camp alongside the Water Meadows, careful to avoid damaging the ecology they were fighting to save."[24] The occupation was 'launched' by Porritt and others chaining themselves across the site.

The Earth First! radicals retreated to set up their camp in the Dongas. They were joined by diverse other groups who adopted the Matabele name for the tracks as a group identity. A small totem pole was passed around and everyone declared themselves to be members of "the Dongas tribe".

Down in the more sedate Water Meadows, "to keep spirits up and maintain an element of stylish humour, the FoE campaign leader Robin Maynard, decided to hold a candlelit dinner... Formal invitations were issued to various members of the Government , but fortunately none of them embarrassed us by accepting or turning up for the superb meal. The press, however, did and photographs in the local and national press recorded one of our more light-hearted and eccentric efforts. Black-tie dress was obligatory, the table was laid with damask linen, and hot food and good wine were served."[25]

When, fortified by their dinner, half a dozen FoE volunteers later chained themselves across the entrance to the motorway construction site, the Department of Transport obtained an injunction against Friends of the Earth that threatened possible confiscation of the organisation's assets if its members did not leave Twyford. The Friends were off like a shot, deserting the earth and heading gladly back to civilisation. Roger Higman explains, "We are not a single issue organisation. We don't just campaign on transport. We ducked out because we were afraid of losing our money and we got pilloried by the rest of the movement for doing so. It was very bitter. But after three or four weeks camping in March, frankly I was very happy to get a bath and a bed."[26]

Rebecca Lush, a Donga, said other members of the tribe were greatly affronted by the Friends' rapid departure, but she was more understanding. "All that happened was Porritt turned up and chained himself to a bit of fencing, and then they got an injunction and fucked off... I found them really nice. Really different political views, obviously. They don't really know what bastards the police are yet. But I didn't until I got involved, and they think changes in the laws save everything... Yet when you look at it they really tried to help... They set up this bizarre 'we are the middle-class, we are representative of middle England' and extremely media-obsessed camp. They found it uncomfortable, but they were fucking there. They used the media skilfully and stopped the works with their own tactics... After three days the police cut this very-easy-to-cut chain and they got slapped with this injunction (meaning) that they could be fined as a company and have their assets taken. I can be gung-ho and say I will go to prison for as long as it takes. That is my individual decision, (but) as a company they have to make decisions... They campaign on everything."[27]

Twyford now acquired a different class of protester. Wall says, "Twyford and later camps provided a magnet for new age travellers and for individuals simply seeking to escape from authority, family commitment or urban unemployment." Lush, returning in the summer, found a traveller sitting in his van watching an episode of the Australian 'soap' Neighbours on a portable television set. Choosing not to join him, she climbed up the Down. "The landscape was very weird: I had never seen anything like it, this bizarre set of gullies, and I thought, 'Wow! This is good'. I got to the top and thought, 'This is even weirder.' There were teepees, and I had never seen a teepee before. It was, like, people lived in teepees, and there were all these very charismatic, bolshy, Donga types... It was interesting and the place was stunning, but nobody talked about the road whatsoever."[28]

Bearing in mind the way the Dongas were to become so heavily identified with the British anti-roads campaign of the early 1990s, it is odd that at first many of them were curiously antipathetic to calls for direct action. In fact, Wall says an informant reported that Earth First! were at one time asked to leave Twyford by the Dongas because they were "upsetting the karma of the place". He reports, "Some Dongas were neo-tribalists with a complex mythological commitment to the land, believing that Twyford Down was the site of King Arthur's Camelot."[29] This idea had been fostered by Christopher Gilham, 50 year old physicist and long time Twyford protester, who told John Vidal, of the *Guardian*: "The enemy has presumed to attack Camelot... A guardian dragon has awakened. Twyford Down is Twyford rising."[30] When Earth First! activists tore down construction site fencing, some of the site workers retaliated by burning down a watchtower and then set light to barricades around the Dongas camp. Lush says, "There was some kind of meeting, and the strongest characters made it clear they did not like direct action... It was antagonising the workers, and you thought, 'Fair enough'. And then you thought: 'Why are we sitting here, in this lovely little camp, if we are not going to stop the road?'"[31]

Summer turned to autumn and sporadic direct action continued with Earth First! activists standing in front of the bulldozers and earth moving machinery. Then as dawn broke on December 9, immortalised as 'Yellow Wednesday' in Donga mythology, a force of yellow jacketed Group 4 security guards moved in to break up the camp. The activists claimed they were subjected to unnecessary violence and that many women protesters were sexually assaulted. Rebecca Lush said, "They were really going for women's breasts, really punching and pinching and twisting and groping. They were also trying to rip clothes off and basically trying to humiliate. It just makes me really angry, being beaten up and sexually assaulted at the same time. They were absolute thugs. We had never come across this type of roughness before. A lot of them were really getting in to hurting people. It's not just sexual assault, it's also sexual harassment as well from security guards who think it's amusing to get a woman on the floor and call her a slut and slag, and stick their pelvis in your face."[32]

David Bellamy, the conservationist well known for his television appearances, said he had never seen violence like it in 20 years of protesting. Even some of the guards themselves were sickened: ten resigned on the first day and 12 the next. John Vidal, of the *Guardian* , was told by one disaffected security man, "When we got on site we were unofficially told to make sure no cameras were watching. Some of our guys went over the top."[33]

When direct action to hinder the cutting of the Down continued after the break-up of the Donga camp, the Department of Transport paid Bray's Detective Agency in Southampton £7,000 to track down 76 protesters, then photograph and identify them so that injunctions might be served. Seven of them, including Lush, Torrance and Simon Fairlie, one of the editors of the *Ecologist* magazine, went on protesting and were jailed for 28 days. As he left to start his sentence in Pentonville Prison, Fairlie said, "We've done this not out of contempt for the law but out of revulsion at the road industry's contempt for democracy. The public inquiry system is blatantly rigged to the advantage of the road lobby. I'm being jailed for walking across Twyford Down, whilst the Department of Transport has been allowed to tear it apart with bulldozers in open defiance of EC law." The protesters were later visited in their cells by none other than Signor Ripa di Meana, now no longer the EC environment commissioner. A month after he had left office, Brussels quietly dropped the Twyford case but kept others on its books. Ripa di Meana said his visit was in "solidarity, sympathy and admiration". As a private citizen of a single Europe, he called on Major's government to reconsider, even at this late stage. "There is greatness in giving up something if you reach a conclusion that a previous decision was wrong," he said.[34]

The trouble was di Meana was scarcely dealing with people capable of greatness. John Major and his 'grey' men would soon be booted into oblivion by the electorate, and the Conservative Party damaged almost beyond repair by its Europhobia.

Twyford was doomed. There were peaceful mass demonstrations, one of which was memorable for a moving scene captured by the TV cameras: a local villager in his 'Sunday best' dark suit holding his young son in his arms walks alone towards a moving bulldozer that is ripping the Down apart. The machine halts, just as a line of tanks had halted in Tiananmen Square in Peking in June 1989 when faced with a similar brave gesture. But that is all it was. When the people had departed, the bulldozers and earth movers continued to defile what had been a beautiful landmark. Led by Davy, their high priest, blowing his horn and (security men, please note) clutching a six-foot wooden staff, the Dongas decamped and faded from the headlines. But they gave notice that they would be back. In a letter to the *Ecologist*, "on behalf of the tribe", Rebecca Lush warned that Twyford Down was just "the symbol of a huge environmental struggle to come: the DoT against the countryside of Britain; the car versus the planet."[35] In this continuing struggle, the battle for Twyford Down would eventually become known as the defeat that won the war.

8

FROM WANSTONIA
TO NIMBYSHIRE

All over Britain in the early 1990s, from the Independent Republic of Wanstonia in the south to the Polok Free State in the north – and all points in between – the Dongas were on the march. There was a beating of drums and a droning of didgeridoos as the tribe came to the aid of Mother Earth. Those points in between included Jesmond Dene, Newcastle. Here, in a noteworthy incident Phil Pritchard, a 22 year old 'veteran' of Twyford Down, climbed into the earthmoving bucket of a bulldozer to protest against what it was doing, and was taken for a ride by the enraged Geordie driver, dangling high above rush-hour traffic. Pritchard hung on for dear life as the driver clashed the bucket against another digger to try to dislodge him, and eventually managed to escape unhurt. There were protests over the A11 in Norfolk, where an ancient pasture called The Lizard – breeding ground for great-crested newts – was scheduled for eradication. Road improvements that threatened parts of the Snowdonia National Park in North Wales were not welcomed in either hillsides or valleys. On the route of the M65 Blackburn bypass, in an abandoned farmhouse near Cuerdon Valley Park, an 'Independent Free Area of Cuerdonia' was set up and candlelit vigils were held. There was the A17 at Leadenham in Lincolnshire, the A39 at Wells in Somerset, the A299 Thanet Way in Kent and the North-South Coventry Link, to name but a few. If the Dongas did not actually halt many road schemes, they did get around the country, had a lot of fun exploring alternative lifestyles, learned how to sabotage the odd JCB, and generally took the opportunity to – as one protester put it to me – "stick two fingers up at the Bill." Most important for the anti-roads campaign as a whole was the media coverage that all of this generated. George Walden of the *Daily Telegraph* reported, "The problem about attending protest meetings against new roads, as I have been doing frequently lately, is finding a place to park."[1]

In a dusty, unlovely part of Wanstead in East London, behind a rusting corrugated iron fence, Lumpy Steve and fellow Dongas have chained themselves to a tree on a patch of waste ground across which, the Department of Transport has decreed, an extension of the M11 should run. For Lumpy Steve this tree is a "symbol of life". In fact, he tells reporters, it possesses the same "life force" as a human being. Lumpy Steve says trees are the lungs of the world – their branches are even shaped like bronchi, aren't they? Cutting them down means the human race doesn't want to breathe no more and, *ergo*, is committing suicide. That's madness, man, you can't go along with that, says Lumpy Steve. Helen, another Donga, recites statistics "like a mantra" to Mick Brown of the *Daily Telegraph*: "Eight hundred ancient monuments under threat, 164 sites of special scientific interest and 80 places of outstanding natural beauty – that's beautiful, sacred green places." Brown writes all this down, then looks around him. "Few would describe Wanstead and Leytonstone as either beautiful or sacred," he notes solemnly, "Yet such is the romantic imagination that Helen and Lumpy can invest even a piece of scrubland behind a corrugated iron fence with an almost sacramental significance."[2]

The Dongas sit in the tree all day. Then, secure in the knowledge that the workmen assigned to cut it down always knock off work at 6pm, they unchain themselves and wander back to their squat on Eastern Avenue for a spot of pasta soup. As soon as they have gone, construction workers on overtime move in and cut down the tree with chainsaws. When he hears the news, Lumpy Steve is quite distraught. "I feel as if they've killed a friend," he says.[3]

The next morning, four miles away in Leyton, an eviction notice is being served on Mick, an elderly sculptor living in a crumbling Edwardian terraced house. Mick has hung banners from the windows, reading 'This Is Not A House, It's A Home'. He has also, ominously, erected makeshift gallows on the roof. Somebody says Mick is prepared to kill himself rather than surrender. Mick says he probably won't go that far. Outside, Dongas and local protesters gather. The latter group includes

Colin Bex, an architect, who is campaigning for the proposed M11 route to be turned into a conservation area. The Dongas explain that they are there to help the locals as "direct action consultants". "The DoT say we're scum, we're ignorant, we're all scroungers," says Helen, "That's the weapon they use to make out we're wrong. But we're none of these things. This is work."[4]

It was work they got better at as time went by. Later that year, on George Green, in that which the Dongas and local activists had by now declared "the Independent Republic of Wanstonia", another tree – a 250 year old sweet chestnut – was declared by a High Court judge to be a legal dwelling place because it had received a letter. When the verdict was announced, the tree received 400 more letters from all over the country congratulating it on its achievement. It was, as John Vidal, of the Guardian, pointed out, a comedy worthy of AP Herbert.

Vidal was there when the tree finally came down. "It has been a life-affirmative drama," he wrote, "People cheerfully sleeping out in trees in freezing temperatures and foul conditions for the principle of a better quality of life for others is unlikely these days. Old women and children helping to push down fences to reclaim nature, shovelling earth back into the frozen ground with their bare hands, seems medieval, yet is a pathetically moving statement about British life today. And right at the end, with a battle raging, people being pulled out of its boughs, arms being broken and tears being shed, the sight of the tree's hangman – the 'cherry picker' lorry – having to be pulled out of the mud was powerful tragi-comedy indeed. But down, in an orgy of violence against people who at all points insisted they would not retaliate, came 250 years of living witness to a community's history in the name of concrete, progress and the motor car. In the coldly logical, economically-oriented world of the state, a tree barely matters – but the cultural image of a leafless old chestnut tree on common land being chainsawed up and then bulldozed over for a road is lasting and easily transmuted to one of defenceless people being bulldozed aside by an insensitive state... There is... a wide sense that post-industrial Britain is on a muddle-headed, destructive development path and that what is being done in the name of old concepts like mobility and economic growth is out dated and out of touch with people's long-term needs."[5]

Meanwhile, north of the border, Dongas arrived to help create the Pollok Free State at Barrhead Woods in Glasgow. In the 1970s, permission had been given for the M77 motorway to cut through green space given to the city by Sir John Stirling Maxwell, founder of the National Trust of Scotland. A three month public inquiry failed to alter the decision, and by 1993 campaigners saw direct action as the only alternative left open to them. The fight continued until 1995 when, a "To Pollok with Love" convoy of cars was driven to the Free State from England. The cars were erected into 'carhenge'; a monument to the folly of the automobile. They were ritually burnt on the rain swept bed of the new motorway, an action that Greenpeace condemned as "environmentally damaging". Eventually, the road was built, though Derek Wall claims the campaign against it "stiffened local resolve on matters of social justice, ecological concern and Scottish working class identity."[6]

ALARM (All London Against the Road Menace) had now evolved into ALARM UK. They coordinated a national fight against road schemes, using computers and fax machines to link protests and direct Dongas – in so much as a Donga can be directed – to places where they were most needed.

Sometimes, it has to be said, campaigners got on better without them. A protest in point was the one in 1993 that actually did save Oxleas Wood in south London. Imagine that it is possible to step back in time from modern day London to the last Ice Age: you would find only one thing unchanged and that would be Oxleas Wood, a mainly oak wood, rich in bird, plant and insect life, at the foot of Shooter's Hill in present day Eltham. Not that Progress had not reared its ugly head. In 1934 a campaign saved the wood from housing development, and it and the neighbouring Shepherdleas Wood had been bought by public subscription for £70,590, and then given 'in perpetuity' to the people of London for their enjoyment.

In the early 1980s, in its inimitable way, the Department of Transport decided there were limits to perpetuity and it was time to disturb the primeval peace of Oxleas Wood. It proposed laying a four lane highway straight through the middle of it. This was necessary, the Department said, to provide a link to the proposed East London River Crossing; a new Thames bridge serving the soon-to-be-developed Docklands area.

In the longest ever public inquiry into any road scheme, lasting from September 1985 to December 1986, 7,000 local people and organisations opposed the scheme. They said the 350 foot wide cutting, besides dividing the wood in two, would destroy at least 500 mature oaks, hornbeams and sweet chestnut trees, along with thousands of smaller trees and bushes. The transport department said only 11.5 per cent of the woods would be destroyed. The objectors, grouped together as People Against the River Crossing (PARC), said the peace and charm of the woods would be lost forever. They claimed that exhaust gases would drive to extinction some of the 33 bird species nesting in them, and bring about levels of noise that would make what was left of Oxleas Wood feel like a giant traffic island. They suggested instead a tunnel, which would add up to £32 million onto the £200 million cost of the road. The Ministries of Transport and the Environment said no to this, and claimed the damage that the road would do to the wood was "environmentally acceptable". As they had to be under the law governing public land, the objectors were offered 25 acres of nearby farmland in exchange for the woodland destroyed by the road. This, said the DoT, could then be planted with trees, and in next to no time it would be just like Oxleas Wood.

People in Eltham turned this down and said Oxleas itself was irreplaceable. They adopted trees in the wood at £5 a tree and pledged they would lie down in front of them to halt their destruction. A mass 'tree-hug' was then held, with the 850 trees earmarked for destruction being embraced by their protectors as the TV cameras whirred. Protestors also complained to Signor Ripa di Meana in Brussels and, as in the case of Twyford Down, he called on the Government to halt work on the river crossing. Whereas the European Commission had dropped opposition to Twyford Down, it stood its ground on Oxleas Wood. Nine objectors also took the case to the High Court, supported by the World Wide Fund for Nature, Friends of the Earth, David Bellamy and Jonathon Porritt. Nigel Pleming QC, appearing for the objectors, said the offer of farmland was unsatisfactory. "It would be a pale pastiche, a kind of Disneyland of woodland," he told the court. The judge, Mr Justice Hutchison, obviously had nothing whatsoever against Mickey Mouse and ruled against the objectors.

It was a severe blow. Among environmentalists nationwide there was a weeping and a wailing and a gnashing of teeth. Roger Higman said, "The judge has given the government extremely wide powers to take our best open spaces and give any land they like in exchange." Then, in what looked like the wood's darkest hour, hope was almost immediately reborn. In Brussels Signor Ripa di Meana's successor, Ioannis Paleokrasas, announced that the European Commission would prosecute the British government in the European Court if the scheme went ahead. A rather laughable face-saving device was then cooked up: the Department of the Environment announced that it was re-examining the Oxleas Wood plan following a suggestion by the British Road Federation. They proposed that the East London River Crossing should end to the south of the Thames at its junction with the A2016 in Thamesmead, instead of taking it to the A2 at Falconwood and thus through Oxleas Wood.

Then on July 7 1993 the Transport Secretary, John MacGregor, announced to the House of Commons that the Oxleas Wood plan had been abandoned. John Gummer, newly appointed Environment Secretary, said the damage to the wood would have been "an unacceptable price to pay" for the road, and even the British Road Federation described the climb-down as "a victory for common sense". Charles Secrett, who had replaced Jonathon Porritt as head of Friends of the Earth, hailed a "victory for wildlife over concrete". Porritt himself said, "The government only gave up on this scheme for political reasons: it realised it simply could not defeat that unique combination of local support plus massive backing from the environment movement." Signor Ripa di Meana arrived at a celebration rally in August and – what else? – planted a tree to commemorate a famous victory.

Meanwhile the Dongas were on the march again, heeding an SOS – Save Our Solsbury. At Solsbury Hill, near Bath, work had already started on the Batheaston-Swainswick bypass. Here the Dongas discovered you got a much better class of protester. The Marchioness of Worcester joined the camp on occasion. Mrs Judith Bentham-Insdale, owner of a Bath art gallery, would drape herself elegantly over JCB diggers as they prepared to uproot trees. And Viscount Norwich would also occasionally confront the bulldozers. "An arrest carries a certain cachet on the dinner party circuit," the *Daily Telegraph* explained.[7]

On Solsbury Hill a large part of the campaign to stop the road was played out high above the ground in Whitecroft, a copse of trees that were due to be felled to make way for the road. Here protesters had built an elaborate network of houses, ones that came with all mod cons. Richard Fairfax's abode, in the fork of a beech, anchored securely 15 metres above the ground was a positive des res, equipped with cooker, pans, candles, carpet, bedding – even a hanging pot of geraniums. Fairfax, a former computer programmer in his early thirties lived there for two months. He told Stephen Venables of the *Daily Telegraph*: "We realised that it was a defendable place so we hung up a helicopter cargo net to make the first tree houses. Then I managed to borrow some climbing equipment and about a week later another climber, Martin Ellis, came from the road protest near Norwich. We managed to interest the Save Our Solsbury campaign in what could be done and show them that a tree protest could be effective. After that donations started to pour in so that we could buy climbing equipment. Then more people – climbers, tree surgeons, outdoors people – turned up to work on the trees." The contractors erected a high steel security fence around the copse but the tree dwellers made a ropeway to the outside world, linked to trees beyond the fence.

Venables described his visit to Whitecroft: "Getting in was an exciting business, inching sideways, feet gripping a wire cable, hands clutching a higher line of braided polypropylene, brain imagining the consequences of a fall. I was glad to be wearing a climbing harness with a safety karabiner clipped into the handrail. Inside the copse I followed my guide from tree to tree. We climbed past a den with a floral sign offering 'Welcome to Sunnyside' then arrived at the biggest wooden platform, the communal kitchen. From there we clipped into the ropes again and crossed to another tree house, where Emma Spenser-Churchill and her fellow protester, Jeremy were tidying up their 7ft by 4ft space, folding up bedding, sweeping the carpet and sorting out their polythene roof. The back wall of their room was a collage of illuminated eco-poems and campaign telephone numbers. Arrayed on the front shelf were tape deck, radio, mobile phone and Tannoy speakers, all powered from a large car battery. Emma explained that they had tried broadcasting acoustic music to the security guards down below 'to improve their attitude'".[8]

In an early skirmish with security men, Martin Ellis slipped from his perch and fell 15 metres to the ground. He was taken to hospital with serious, multiple injuries. Then two security men – known to the protesters as "blue hats" – threatened to climb into Whitecroft using the ropeway from the trees beyond the security fencing. As they did so, Emma's voice came over the Tannoy: "Will you please get down from the trees. Do not try to cross the wires: you do not have safety harnesses and we do not want any more accidents. We have spoken on the phone to your supervisor who says you have no authority to be up here." Venables reported: "By now it was dark. The gentle rustling of leaves was shattered by four generators roaring into life and the whole tree community was flooded with white light, glaring from tall pylons. Morale lifted at 10.45pm when Richard announced on the intercom to 'base' outside the perimeter: 'The situation has changed completely. The three blue hats who performed this rash action have now climbed back to the ground. I think that security have realised it was all rather silly.'" But well organised though it all was, shortly after Venables' visit, the protesters were pulled out of their trees, which were then sawn down.

Elsewhere at the bypass site Bel Mooney, author of children's books and wife of broadcaster Jonathan Dimbleby, forsook her nearby home in a converted Georgian vicarage to live with the Dongas for a week in a yurt (a Mongolian bell-tent), during which she went on a well publicised hunger strike in protest at the bypass. She had decorated the yurt with kilim rugs which usually hung in her study. She had a small table, some folding chairs and a tape recorder so that she could listen to Gregorian chants in the evening. When not thus occupied, Mooney would read her stories to the dreadlocked Dongas.

She told *Sunday Telegraph* reporter Sandra Barwick that she just could not understand why she had been ridiculed by female columnists in the tabloid press. "I wonder why these women should find it necessary to deride me with such vitriol for saying, 'I don't want this road. I want to save the trees.' I think those appalling female columnists can't bear someone like me being so committed, sincere. I don't know whether someone moving out of line like I did makes them uneasy and the only way to cope with it is this shocking bitching. If they met me in London in my little cocktail frock they'd think I was fine, wouldn't they?"⁹

Barwick said she rather thought they would. Though she did confess to being somewhat taken aback when Mooney told her that she had recently driven to London and back just for a drinks party. Mooney said, "I think you should treat it like Australians do, and people who live in Vermont – drive for two hours for dinner. People in England should be like that." When Barwick pointed out that this seemed a little out of place coming from an anti-roads protester, Mooney replied, not at all and said she was not even against the bypass as such. Rather, it was the scale of it – in some places, she claimed, it would be wider than the M5. "The country as a whole is being eaten up by roads," said Mooney, "You simply can't bear it. If someone tells me about a new one – there's one in Grimsby – I simply physically can't bear it. I get a knot in my system. But you simply have to go on." She said that the last time she had been shopping, a local greengrocer had given her a bunch of flowers because of her involvement in the road protest. "I burst into tears."¹⁰

Unhappily, Mooney fell out with the Dongas when, after the Solsbury Hill protest had been routed, she refused to allow some of them to set up a camp on a nearby field owned by herself and Dimbleby. As a result she was accused of that most heinous of crimes, Nimbyism – from the acronym NIMBY, Not In My Back Yard. Again she was pilloried in the press. "People can say what they like," she told Wendy Holden of the *Daily Telegraph*, "I have done more than enough. Over the months, I have provided a great deal of food, a lot of clothes and equipment. I allowed people into my home to have baths. I lived with them for a week and went on hunger strike. If I let them camp on my husband's fields, not only would I be divorced, but I would be pilloried by the local people for going too far. I don't believe that local communities or local farmers should feel they have a moral right to find these people a field, but now I am being pilloried for saying so." She said the land was used to rear organic cattle and grow wild flowers. Dennis Wakefield, a local newsagent who was in favour of the bypass, said, "It all boils down to the fact that she is a Nimby. We are delighted that the protesters have been ordered off the site and it is all over now bar the shouting."¹¹

Batheaston was indeed lost. Traffic now thunders through an ugly cutting straight through Solsbury Hill. But by now the Department of Transport, under the lacklustre John MacGregor, was facing a massive Tory revolt against its plans.

Among these was a scheme to turn parts of the M25 into a 14 lane highway, making it the widest motorway outside the US. Steven Norris, Parliamentary Under Secretary for Roads at the time, explains, "The idea of expanding the M25 seemed pretty logical. We'd started of course with six lanes. We'd already widened to eight and they'd already become congested. We needed some more capacity, so 'Why don't we build three lanes each way of new capacity and – bingo! – we've got 14 lanes.'"[12]

The motorway ran through hitherto solid Conservative territory and opposition to the scheme threatened to split the Party. Even people who were unaffected by the plan itself were appalled. Alan Whitfield, who was now Director of the Road Programme Division at the Department of Transport, says, "It wasn't the professional opposition that made me realize we'd gone a step too far, it was the general social reaction that I met wherever I went, whether it was at home at a dinner party or whether it was at a gathering of friends. People would say, 'You're not serious about this 14 lanes, are you?' It was just a step – at that time – too far."[13]

By November 1993 after a year of protests, the writing was on the wall. Or rather in the Conservative *Daily Telegraph*, as it printed an article headlined "Time to turn the tide of tarmac".

"In the Tory heartland of the south of England, John MacGregor, the Transport Secretary, has the beginnings of a revolt on his hands... about the vision – or lack of it – behind transport policy itself," the paper said. "Fellow Tories are now asking whether the £23 billion road building programme should be the Government's only plan for accommodating our future transport needs. A string of bypasses planned for unspoilt parts of the Chilterns has been revealed to be part of a four-lane Euro-expressway thundering from Felixstowe to Swindon. Villagers in Oxfordshire and Buckinghamshire rise in protest. Lord Bullock, author of Hitler: A Study in Tyranny, rails against the Department of Transport's 'hidden agenda'. The impression is given that the DoT knows its policies are unpopular and is trying to implement them by stealth."[14]

The article pointed out that when the Euro-expressway through Oxfordshire was debated late at night in the Commons, observers had noted the presence of two ministers: the Education Secretary, John Patten, and the Environment Minister, Tony Baldry, whose constituencies were affected. Tory antennae were twitching over the M25 widening plan, said the *Daily Telegraph* article. Local people "know more cars mean more noise, more urbanisation, more pollution and ultimately more congestion. People want the option not to drive.

"Accommodating the DoT's projected doubling of traffic growth over the next 30 years will make American-style 12 and 14 lane super-highways inevitable. And that will mean more unwanted development on what remains of the green and pleasant land. Besides the widened M25, there are plans for a 14 lane section of the M62 in Manchester. Where next? Surrey, the first county to be affected by the widening of the M25, has asked the High Court to grant a judicial review of Mr MacGregor's decision to treat the widening – for the purposes of a public inquiry – as a series of separate schemes instead of one project." The paper said people in Runnymede, home of the Magna Carta, were complaining that they had been effectively disenfranchised from making any changes to M25 widening.

"Do we have to go on covering England in concrete and indulge the motor car? Is damage to the quality of life for people in Surrey, Oxfordshire or Manchester necessary for a healthy economy?"[15]

In August 1994, MacGregor was replaced as Transport Secretary by the more capable Brian Mawhinney. By now the Transport Department was under threat from two quarters on its own side of the fence: The Department for the Environment, worried about Britain's inability to meet the targets for reducing emission levels agreed at the United Nations Earth Summit, held in Rio de Janeiro, Brazil, in 1992; and the Treasury, anxious as always to reduce public spending and finding the roads programme a progressively easier target for cuts. Two hammer blows fell in late 1994. The Royal Commission on Environmental Pollution, comprising some of Britain's top scientists, called for a halving of the roads programme and investment in alternative transport. Then SACTRA, the Standing Advisory Committee on Trunk Roads Assessment, produced evidence that, far from solving traffic problems, new roads simply generated more traffic.

Steven Norris, Mawhinney's deputy, says, "It became clear to me that you simply could not 'predict and provide'. You simply could not allow travel and traffic to grow at their own, unrestricted rate without any concern from government and simply accept as your task concreting over enough of Britain to allow that traffic to move. It simply wasn't socially acceptable, it wasn't politically acceptable and, bluntly, it wasn't intellectually acceptable. Where on earth were you going to stop?"[16]

Mawhinney dropped seven road schemes and ordered "extra assessment" for 270 of the 360 outstanding schemes.

As ALARM UK said at the time, "None of this means that road-building is a thing of the past, but all political parties are looking to scale it down considerably and are looking at other ways of dealing with the country's transport problems... A transport revolution is taking place."

One last major confrontation remained.

9

THE DONGAS' LAST STAND

Roundheads and Cavaliers fought two battles near the Berkshire town of Newbury during the English Civil War. The prize then was liberty. More than 300 years on, when the Dongas took on the might of the road-building establishment for what was billed as The Third Battle of Newbury, it was on behalf of colonies of dormice, bats and nightjars. These – along with the two Civil War battlegrounds – were due to be wiped out by the nine mile A34 bypass around the town; part of a major Euro-route.

The bypass scheme had been in the headlines for years and in 1994 had been put on hold by Transport Secretary Brian Mawhinney. By the end of 1995, the Conservatives were disastrously low in the opinion polls, and a general election was looming in which a revitalised 'new' Labour was poised to take command under its young leader Tony Blair. Mawhinney realised that he did not have a great deal to lose and gave the go-ahead for what the arboreally named Tony Juniper, of Friends of the Earth, called "a dinosaur of a road scheme, one of the most destructive in the government's road programme".

By January 1996, when work was scheduled to begin, the Dongas were well dug in. Along the path of the bypass there were nine different camps with names like Tree Pixie Village and Granny Ash. Other, more militant anti-roads campaigners were actually underneath the route, burrowing out a network of tunnels, some extending 150 feet into the clay, while high above ground they created a colony of 60 connected tree houses. Heaven only knows what the threatened nightjars, bats and dormice made of all this activity.

The tunnels were a new idea, which had their origin in

ecological protests against tree-felling in the rainforests of New South Wales. George Marshall, an English Earth First! activist who had visited Australia, is thought to have brought the technique back to England. The idea was that when the security guards moved in, last-ditch protesters in the tunnels would chain themselves to concrete blocks set in oil barrels and hold up construction work until they could be cut free and manoeuvred to the surface. Hum the Hawk, a veteran Donga campaigner, aged 27, explained: "Once the bailiffs come in and they start cutting down trees, it is inevitable that they will move us out eventually. It is a case of holding on for as long as possible to heighten awareness."[1]

The protesters were armed with a formidable array of high tech weapons: mobile telephones, pagers, CB radios and battery-powered laptop computers connected to the Internet. More importantly they also had one of the best chefs in the business. David Lenaghan, aged 28, from Chichester, West Sussex, had been working with Albert Roux as a commis chef before defecting to Newbury. Using camp fires and equipment that included a 12 gallon cauldron dating from the Crimean War nicknamed 'Puffing Billy', from his 'kitchen' in a forest camp on a budget of just £60 a day, Lenaghan provided the 200 protesters with a breakfast of porridge, fresh fruit and nuts, washed down with barley cordial. After they had done battle with the security guards, the tribe could look forward to a 'menu gastronomique' that on one occasion comprised six-vegetable Thai stir fry in chilli sauce, potato latka, three bean soup, cooked beetroot and fresh fruit salad. Lenaghan said he had got bored creating buffets for London businessmen and felt at Newbury he was making "a positive contribution to a positive cause." He said, "I hated working in London; the pecking order in the kitchen, the egos, the ingratitude. Here, people thank you for cooking." All that the security guards had to look forward to were chicken pieces, beef burgers, bread, cabbage and eggs, washed down with lashings of tomato ketchup and fizzy drinks.[2]

In Newbury itself, right next door to the headquarters of the district council, which supported the bypass, Friends of the Earth set up an office to help coordinate the fight.

There was much debate in the town on the forthcoming

battle. David Rendel, Newbury's Liberal Democrat MP, claimed pollution in the centre was three times the national average and said the bypass was badly needed. He said 50,000 vehicles passed through the town each day, 19 per cent of them lorries. "The people of Newbury know what the problems of the current road are and that is why they strongly support the bypass scheme," said Rendel. "It undoubtedly will do some environmental damage to the land to the west of Newbury, but that has to be balanced with the huge pollution problems that the current road is causing in Newbury."

However, some local businessmen claimed the bypass was being built in the wrong place and said it should be on the eastern side of the town, closer to local industry. Adrian Foster-Fletcher, head of a local recruitment agency, said: "I am totally opposed to the bypass, particularly the route. It is disruptive and divisive." John Bentham, another businessman, said, "Basically, we are talking about the destruction of beautiful English countryside. If the bypass has to be built they should consider the tunnel option or other solutions."[3]

Rendel said he remained "totally convinced" that most local people and businesses wanted the bypass. They certainly did not want the Dongas. Yvonne Northcott, a 51 year old school secretary, said, "These people are lucky to have so much time to spend up trees. They think the countryside is so beautiful but they don't seem to care about the pollution in the town." While displaying that conciliatory spirit that can only come with age, Victor Gregory, aged 70, said if the protesters refused to come down from the trees the construction workers should saw them down anyway.

On January 9, Day One, undaunted and well fortified with David Lenaghan's five-star porridge, the Dongas sallied bravely forth at 5.30am, taking the police and security men completely by surprise. They set up tripods on the roads leading to Abbots Farm, where 400 security guards were billeted; blocking the roads until 1.30pm, when on compassionate grounds they allowed an ambulance through – one of the guards had injured his back, another had suffered an epileptic fit. By then the Department of Transport called off work for the day. The jubilant Dongas went off to enjoy a spicy stir fry, leaving the disconsolate guards to chomp morosely on beef burgers. Rowan, Dug and

Simon, the heroes who had manned the tripods, were toasted with soya milk cocktails.

At this stage of the game it was all very friendly. Tom Riall, area manager for Reliance Security, admitted, "They have taken us by surprise this morning but the guys are all resigned to things like this happening. We actually enjoy quite a good relationship with the protesters." Such sweetness and light was not to be found everywhere, though. Andy Drury, a 'legal observer' for the campaign, said a local farmer was threatening to shoot protesters and stampede his cattle through their ranks. An unnamed local resident, who obviously had a lot in common with the afore-quoted Mr Gregory, told *The Times* the police should pull down the tripods and "take a flamethrower to the lot of them".[4]

Day Two started badly for the Dongas. Some 150 guards resplendent in helmets and luminous yellow jackets fell in either side of a mechanical digger and marched alongside it to Great Penn Wood, which was due to be cleared. A small encampment of about a dozen Dongas was easily brushed aside, and hedges and trees flattened as the digger started work. The Dongas were down, but not out. They used mobile telephones and CB radios to call up reinforcements, then they hurled themselves at the digger, forcing it to stop work. As the reinforcements arrived, the guards fought to drive them back, linking arms in a tight circle, but two Dongas managed to get beneath the digger's claws, clinging on for dear life, while others planted themselves in muddy holes from which trees had been uprooted. One protester and one security guard suffered leg injuries in this confrontation. The security guards radioed for reinforcements of their own, only to discover that another detachment of Dongas had attacked the base of the bus company used to ferry them to the site, forcing it to recall its coaches. Work was abandoned for the day. The Dongas cheered and shouted, "Two-nil, two-nil!"

Forty-eight hours into the Third Battle of Newbury, little more than an hour's work had been completed, with only 50 small trees cleared. David Rendel was outraged. Obviously choosing his words carefully, the MP described it as "extraordinary" that the demonstrators had won the day. Inspector Frank Connor, in charge of the police, was defensive. He said, "It is not a police job to move these people out, it is a matter for the security guards. The main thing is that nobody gets injured."

The protesters were quizzed by the media on their victorious tactics. Rebecca Lush, by now a seasoned campaigner after her initial involvement at Twyford Down, said modestly that there were no leaders and strategy was just worked out around camp fires or in local pubs. "Any meetings we have are very informal," she explained, "We just bash out ideas. It's imagination and ingenuity." Simon Festing, of Friends of the Earth, said the campaigners were inspired by Gandhi.

Day Three saw another Donga victory. The contractors got their digger working again but, with too few security guards to form a ring around it at a distance safe enough for clearance work to begin, work was called off at 9.30am. Explaining the lack of manpower, Reliance Security revealed that it had been forced to send home 200 guards after torrential rain had washed out their tented village during the night.

Keith Lock, Liberal Democrat leader of Newbury District Council, was apoplectic. Angrily demanding extra guards and a more active police role, he said he was worried that work on the bypass would not be completed before the nesting season; if this happened it would have to be halted to allow the nightjars a fair crack of the whip. "The whole operation is a shambles," said Lock, "The police may have to take a stronger line. I think more resources are needed to create a bigger screen around the workmen."[5]

On Day Four, obviously stung to action by his words, the police got tougher. They arrested 34 protesters for aggravated trespass under the Criminal Justice Bill. The contractors also changed their tactics, taking the Dongas by surprise. Abandoning attempts to use the digger, they sent in mobile chainsaw gangs. Work was disrupted at one site for about an hour as protesters climbed trees and formed circles round the contractors' vehicles. Elsewhere workmen felled 200 beech trees and were confronted by only 30 or so doleful Dongas while they did it.

A protester suffered head injuries and was taken to hospital. The Dongas said he had been hit by a security guard; the police said he fell. The police admitted to having pushed a woman demonstrator over a barbed wire fence. Inspector Connor said, "We are quite happy for people to protest lawfully, go into fields and carry placards but the contractors are also entitled to do their job and if they are stopped, people will be arrested for aggravated trespass. We gave repeated warnings. You had trees falling in a confined area so the arrests were for the protesters' own safety."[6]

Simon Festing said he was concerned by the more aggressive approach. "This was politically motivated," he said. "It means in effect, that the police are taking a side in the debate. I think it is the first stage leading to violence by police and security guards. The two seem to be hand in hand and the approach was definitely more aggressive."

David Rendel was jubilant; the message appeared to have got through to the government that the contractors needed better protection. He said, "While lawful protest needs to be protected, the law of the land must be obeyed and I am pleased that the police are acting against illegal protests."

But the next day, the Dongas won a small but important battle: the right to receive their social security payments at Newbury. The Transport Department had called for the payments to be withdrawn because the protesters were not "available for work". But a team from the Benefits Agency who visited Newbury declared afterwards that – as in the case of the Wanstead tree – the camps were acceptable addresses for the delivery of Giro cheques.

With this worry off their minds, the tribe threw itself back into the campaign with renewed ferocity. On January 16, one week in, there were fierce clashes as campaigners chained themselves to machinery and climbed trees that were about to be cut down at three different sites. Police made 20 arrests.

Armed with names of protesters compiled by Bray's detective agency, which first became involved in identifying campaigners at Twyford Down, the Highways Agency said it would ask the High Court to grant it possession orders on four Donga sites at Newbury. This meant it would be able to clear the camps in advance of work starting.

Tension was rising. There was no talk of Gandhi's influence now, much less of the security guards' "good relationship" with the protesters. Instead, *The Times* reported that the police were concerned about the role of highly organised radical groups, such as Earth First! at Newbury. They claimed Earth First! had set up a 'safe camp' for protesters arriving from other parts of the country, and had established something menacingly called a 'destruction hotline'. The paper said the group's newsletter bore the motto "breaking something is the only way" in – would you believe it? – Welsh. *The Times* said Earth First! described itself as "based on a concept of non-hierarchical organisation, direct action and the empowerment of individuals to confront the ecological catastrophe facing our planet".[7]

At Newbury, in addition to tunnelling, another Earth First! tactic that was adopted was the driving of spikes into trees about to be felled. This makes felling extremely dangerous to chainsaw operators, who might easily suffer severe injury if the chain hits the metal and goes berserk. This technique in ecological sabotage appears to have been the invention of Edward Abbey. In his foreword for the US Earth First! manual *Ecodefense*, the novelist wrote, "No good American should ever go into the woods again without... a hammer and a few pounds of 60-penny nails... You won't hurt the trees; they'll be grateful for the protection; and you may save the forest. My Aunt Emma back in West Virginia has been enjoying this pleasant exercise for years. She swears by it. It's good for the trees, it's good for the woods, it's good for the earth, and it's good for the human soul."[8]

For an ecologist, Abbey had some curious ideas: one of The Monkey Wrench Gang, while crusading against the consumer society, litters the highway with empty beer cans. "He was indeed a menace to other drivers but justified himself in this way: If you don't drink, don't drive. If you drink, drive like hell. Why? Because freedom, not safety, is the highest good. Because the public roads should be wide open to all – children on tricycles, little old ladies in Eisenhower Plymouths, homicidal lesbians driving forty-ton Mack tractor trailers. Let us have no favorites, no licenses, no goddamn rules for the road. Let every freeway be a free-for-all."[9]

Rage against what man is doing to the world takes many forms, some rational, others less so. It can be difficult for the individuals concerned to explain. As the drama at Newbury was unfolding, Lucy Pearce, a young Exeter University graduate, daubed her body with anti-car slogans and stripped naked in Coventry Cathedral. Miss Pearce, whose mother had been killed in a road accident when she was five, had gone to Coventry from a Donga camp against a road scheme on the A30 near Exeter.

After the incident, which left the aged congregation in a state of shock and, of course, hit the headlines of all Britain's tabloid newspapers, Miss Pearce told *The Times*, "This morning I went out and got all the papers to see what they made of me. They don't seem to understand I was emulating Lady Godiva or what the protest was really about. They just wanted to show my body. Everybody wants to know about my mother dying and my nephew having asthma but it's about much more than that. My mother did die in a car crash when I was five but it is not something I really want to talk about, though I suppose it must have something to do with it all. I suppose I have been an environmentalist ever since I can remember. I always felt this way, regardless of what was happening in my personal life. My nephew's situation does worry me, though. Even the Government's Chief Medical Officer has admitted car pollution is a secondary cause of breathing difficulties. During the hot summer we were all advised it was dangerous for asthmatic children to go outside because of the high levels of pollution. How would you like to tell your child he can't run outside because of the car?"[10]

Back at Newbury, on January 17, a huge influx of security men allowed the contractors to complete their first full day of work since the battle began. More than 30 people were arrested. Five days later the number of guards had risen to 500 – they outnumbered protesters by about four to one. With 10 per cent of the route now cleared, the campaigners admitted they were unable to halt work. Extremists now used another of the highly questionable Edward Abbey's 'ecotage' techniques: they cut a brake pipe on one of the coaches carrying the security guards. Guards also claimed they had been urinated upon, quite literally from a great height, by some of the tree-dwellers. They reported several instances of 'spiked' trees, which the Highways Agency described mildly as a "nasty" tactic. The agency said the level of protest had tailed off but claimed a "campaign of intimidation" was being waged against guards and contractors. "We accept people's right to protest but we had hoped it would remain non-violent," said a spokesman.

The fight moved to London. With demonstrators parading

outside, carrying placards reading "Cut Traffic Not Trees" and "No Newbury Bypass", The High Court predictably ruled that the government had the right to clear camps, tunnels and treetop homes along the route of the bypass in advance of clearance work. The campaigners argued that, although they were trespassing, the Highways Agency had no right to evict them: compulsory purchase orders for the land were invalid as an environmental impact assessment, required under European law, had not been carried out. Mr Justice Collins said this was not needed because consent for the bypass was given before that law took effect in 1988. He refused an adjournment and said the time for a judicial review was "long gone". The issue had to be resolved quickly, said the Judge, because of the cost of delays. "We are all paying for it," he said and awarded costs against the six protesters named in the action. He also refused them leave to appeal, and turned down a request for an injunction stopping work on the bypass. Helen Anscomb, one of the six, who earned just £9,000 a year as a part-time teacher, said afterwards it was "outrageous" that she might be forced to meet costs. "I think the British people will think this is a lowdown thing," she told reporters. "I think there is tremendous public concern here." Another protester, who asked not to be named, said, "I'm feeling pretty disappointed with the whole system. This is supposed to be a court of law and justice but there doesn't seem to be much justice down here today. We will be ready for them when they come. They will have to get us out of the trees and that's not going to be easy."[11]

However not all members of the British Establishment felt like Mr Justice Collins. Lady Jeanine Barber, wife of Sir David Barber, third baronet of Greasley, visited the Newbury camps with her friend Louisa Mollo, wife of John Mollo – twice an Oscar-winner for his costume designs for the films *Star Wars* and *Gandhi*. These two ladies distributed home-made cake to the protesters. Penny Wark reported in the *Sunday Times*: "Being seen to protest is becoming socially acceptable among the hunting, shooting and fishing classes. Only last week, Rupert Legge, son of the formidable Raine (formerly Spencer), Comtesse de Chabrun, and his wife Victoria, astonished a London soirée by announcing that they would call in at Newbury on their way home to Bath. 'But the racing is at Kempton,' replied a perplexed chum. Then Charlie Brooks, the debonair Old Etonian and racehorse trainer, declared himself against the bypass. 'People are getting pretty vociferous at dinner parties round here,' he said. Lord Palumbo and Sir Terence Conran have also pledged their support for the protesters and the Duke of Wellington sent a decent £50. And the Marchioness of Worcester, the former Tracy Ward, has become such an ardent patron of everything green that she hosts environmental salons at her London home and bicycles in a gas mask bearing the message: 'I am being poisoned'. 'Newbury is a very hot issue,' confirmed Celestria Noel, daughter of the Earl of Gainsborough and social editor of *Harpers & Queen*. 'The upper classes have always been country lovers, but now they are prepared to get involved.'"[12]

Not all of them were on the side of the angels, however. When he heard about the protesters tunnelling under the bypass route, the Earl of Carnarvon, racing manager to the Queen, suggested, "Why not send ferrets down after them?"

Three security guards 'defected' to the Donga camp. Brette Shepherd said, "It was all too much so I have given it up." Stephen Ray said he had been sacked after telling police about an incident in which one of his superiors assaulted a female protester. And Graham Wanstall said he had been demoted as a cameraman for filming a senior guard hitting a protester.

There was an interlude in which 4,000 people took part in a peaceful march against the bypass, organised by Friends of the Earth and Greenpeace. They included the actress Maggie Philbin, who said, "I felt I just couldn't sleep in my bed unless I got out there and said what I thought. I know Newbury has a desperate traffic problem but I don't want Newbury to be ten years down the line with the same problem having lost all this countryside."

Then, as evictions continued and work on the bypass proceeded, a feeling of desperation set in. On February 12, a group of masked activists raided the Newbury offices of the construction company Tarmac Roadstone. Thirty employees watched helplessly as the protesters disabled computers, fax machines and telephones, rifled files and threw a fire extinguisher through a window. A caretaker who tried to resist the invasion was slightly hurt. A police spokesman described the incident as "mob rule".

Back at the site, the protesters were clutching at straws, or rather snails. In an appeal to the High Court against their evictions, they claimed to have discovered the extremely rare Desmoulins' Whorl Snail (Verdigo moulinsiana). No bigger than a breadcrumb, this snail had been living since the last Ice Age in what was now the Rickety Bridge camp site. The protesters asked the High Court to allow them to stay on the land to protect it. Mr Justice Sedly dismissed their appeal but asked the Department of Transport to give an undertaking that it would consult with English Nature before clearing the snails. Anxious to prove that they were equally kind to animals, the contractors said they were luring badgers away from the route with peanut butter sandwiches. They also said they were fitting any badger setts they found with swing doors that allowed the animals to leave but not to return (although personally I have always found swing doors a bit of a nightmare for allowing you to do the reverse). The contractors claimed to have relocated hundreds of noctule and pipistrelle bats, and the Highways Agency said spans on four bridges carrying the bypass over the Kennet and Lambourn valleys would be widened to allow wildlife, such as otters, more room. And the dormice? Usually reliable sources said they just slept through it all.

Meanwhile it was crunch time, and not just for Desmoulins' Whorl snails. In a series of pre-dawn raids, bailiffs and police – led by Nicholas Blandy, under-sheriff of Berkshire – flushed protesters out of tree houses and sealed off tunnels. Blandy was bullish. "We are not going to get stopped," he said, "The road is going to get through, which is as it should be." But there were violent clashes and it took days to clear the area. One Donga, naked except for a pair of red rubber gloves and a coating of Vaseline, swung from branch to branch pursued by the bailiffs in a high-hoist hydraulic platform or 'cherrypicker'. Blandy and his men were also somewhat taken aback by the sudden appearance in the treetops of a woad-daubed 'druid' calling himself Arthur Uther Pendragon, who put a curse on them.

Peter Bukowski, a professional climber from Sheffield who was earning £2,000 a week to help clear the tree houses, resigned shortly afterwards; less because of the druid's curse, and more because fellow mountaineers in his home town were threatening to ostracise him for giving the sport a bad name.

Chris Plant, another climber, who came to Newbury to persuade Bukowski to quit, said, "There's a big reaction in the climbing world against working for the bailiffs... Climbing has traditionally been very environmentally aware. We used to have to hold mass protests to get access to common land so I personally feel an affinity with the road protesters."[13]

As the trees were slowly felled, Christine Crerar, who lives near the route, used a loud-hailer to ask police, "What does it feel like when a tree goes down? You are only puppets. You didn't join the police force to watch this. None of you did. You have got to live with this for the rest of your lives." She went on to tell them about the Mary Hare School for the Deaf on a nearby hilltop, attended by her niece Alicia, aged 12. "There is a school for deaf children at the top of that hill. They learn classical music by laying their heads on the table and listening to the vibrations. This route is going through the grounds of their school. The noise of the traffic will stop them from hearing low sounds. They will not be able to talk to each other in the playground. You cannot tell me you agree with that and condone it. If you don't care about that, there is something wrong with you, you don't belong in the police force."[14]

In revenge for their eviction, protesters sought to disturb Blandy's slumbers by climbing onto the roof of his house one night and broadcasting the sound of chainsaws felling trees through a loudspeaker. Unfortunately, the sheriff was out at the time. Demonstrations continued. On one memorable occasion police lines were breached by a pantomime cow, and later at Andover magistrates court, the front and rear ends of the animal denied charges of aggravated trespass.

On April 3, with the felling of the last five trees, it was all over. A protester described the feeling: "As the last tree hit the ground, most of the security guards cheered. I didn't understand this; even without understanding our perspective, it meant they were now out of a job... As for us now, we sat down. We weren't enraged or furious. We were subdued, wiped out. It's a weird set-up where those who care most about environmental destruction are those who see so much of it at first hand."[15] The cost to the taxpayer of evicting protesters and protecting the clearance teams was estimated at £4 million. There had been a total of 767 arrests. That summer when the road was finally opened, it was with no celebration or ceremony whatsoever. Just before midnight the last bulldozers and earth moving machines were loaded onto lorries and driven away. Then traffic cones and barriers were quietly removed. Finally the last of the yellow jacketed men walked silently to their cars and drove away into the darkness without looking back.

TODAY

"Bonnie, you think we're alone? I'll bet – listen, I'll bet right this very minute there's guys out in the dark doing the same kind of work we're doing. All over the country, little bunches of guys in twos and threes, fighting back."
"You're talking about a well-organized national movement."
"No I'm not. No organization at all. None of us knowing anything about any other little bunch. That's why they can't stop us."

– Edward Abbey, The Monkey Wrench Gang

10
SWAMPY, GENERAL DISASTER, RENT-A-MOB – WHO ARE THESE GUYS?

The Press, which by its very nature loves to pigeon-hole and categorise, is quite at a loss when it comes to the eco-warrior. One of the problems is that the average eco-warrior does not exactly court publicity. Quite the reverse. A certain reticence is induced when living on the fringes of polite society, perhaps dependent on the DHS for your wherewithal, and maybe using banned substances for your kicks. Even the more 'respectable' of the tribe tend to be suspicious of people with notebooks. Derek Wall tells of a meeting with ecological activists in a field somewhere in the Home Counties. "I mean we're a long way from anywhere and suddenly this bloke comes along who's a spy and not even a good spy. It was just so obvious."[1] Wall also claims to have been approached by a uniformed police officer of the Metropolitan force's Forward Intelligence Team (FIT) as he and his young son left an Earth First! protest in central London. "Presumably because I was last to leave, I was the likely guide to any stragglers looking for action. He asked if he could accompany us. My answer was non-committal. He followed us on the Circle and Northern (Underground) Lines all the way to Camden in distant north London before realising we were not travelling to meet Earth First!ers for the next stage of their protest: instead we had a brief shopping trip to make before going home."[2]

Wall says: "FIT officers aim to identify and make contact with key activists in Earth First! and the anti-roads movement. The FIT are uniformed and open about their intentions. This officer had attempted to engage me with detailed questions about my involvement and opinions. He had been particularly keen to learn if I'd attended an earlier action where 7,000 protesters, as opposed to the thirty or forty we had been earlier, had held a massive illegal free party on the M41, the normally busy London motorway."[3]

Action Update, the Earth First! newsletter, reported the creation of the FIT thus: "The 12-strong team can now be seen on every sizeable action around the country. They aim to build a 'rapport with (key) activists so that people likely to provoke disorder can be identified early in an event'. The aim of this is to split the direct action movement from within. They are relying on people talking to them or simply grassing other activists up."[4]

Even when the journalist finally extracts quotes out of an eco-warrior, these may not be exactly palatable for a middle-class readership. Take the following example: "It was a fucking awful night, it was horizontal rain coming down, it was freezing... I happened to get up in the tree anyway because no one else was up there, and I was concerned that the Old Bill were going to steal a march on people and come early. I had started guarding the bottom of the ladder to make sure other people had access, and then I went up and parked myself up there... Come three in the morning and the Old Bill come, you know, swarming in, hundreds of the bastards."[5] Or: "I just think like we've got to get shot of all these fucking lethal lumps of metal charging round the streets, killing people, poisoning the air. Listen, if I can help, you know, like putting a dent in the side of Mrs Average's new Rover with my steel-capped Docs when I've done a few lagers, I feel OK about that. They're all trashing the planet, man, these nice ordinary average people. Maybe I can help them to think, maybe it helps wake them up."[6]

Yet there are eco-warriors out there with an appeal to that all-important middle-class readership: "I did quite a bit of my growing up in Yorkshire, in the Dales... I wouldn't call it wilderness but... in this country it's quite a nice wild area and animals are my big passion in life. I wanted to be a vet when I grew up, and all that kind of stuff."[7]

The 1997 British general election campaign would prove quite a watershed for the media. Realising that the Tories were on the way out and probably for a good long time, some of the most unlikely newspapers began to cosy up to Tony Blair and his team. The realisation that road protests were attracting more and more middle and even upper class participants, also caused a revision of attitudes. The time had finally come for a Donga media star. Daniel Hooper, known to his friends as Swampy, was The Chosen One.

Swampy's rise to stardom began when he emerged to cheers, smiling crookedly and blinking in the arc lights after spending 167 hours in a tunnel protesting against an extension to the A30 at Fairmile in Devon. He was feted as "the crusty with a conscience", the eco-warrior that *Daily Mail* women readers would most like to mother. Swampy's rise to fame was positively meteoric. One minute he was crawling around in the mud of Big Momma, the tunnel under Fairmile, the next he was appearing on television, modelling Giorgio Armani fashions, and negotiating an advance of £40,000 with the Fourth Estate publishing company to write The Eco-Terrorist's Handbook. Victoria Barnsley, of Fourth Estate, said this would be the Sloane Ranger's Handbook for the 1990s: "There will be tips on building tunnels, cleaning tunnels and the trickier question of romance in tunnels."[8]

Swampy even became something of an eco-statesman and began issuing eco-soundbites. "I am asked if I think of myself as a hero. My answer is that all of us fighting schemes like this are heroes," he told reporters at Fairmile. John Watts, outgoing Tory Roads Minister, caused uproar when he said he would be happy to see Swampy buried in concrete. When Swampy was asked what he thought about Watts' comments, he replied, "What the minister said was stupid and thoughtless." He added, "The man is a prat."[9]

At one point, Swampy seemed to be about to enter the political fray himself. He offered – if someone would put up the necessary £500 deposit – to stand at Blackley, North Manchester, against Labour candidate Graham Stringer, chairman of Manchester Airport, whose plans for a new runway were provoking a new environmental protest.[10]

Then he admitted he had just been joking. After tunnelling with other protesters at Manchester for a while, Britain's favourite 'mole' went back to the A30 at Fairmile, where he dug a new tunnel and stayed in it for seven days. By this time the Labour government had been elected and when he came out of the tunnel, Swampy faced the cameras. "Being back here raises the issue of how people's taxes are being wasted," he said. "I started digging here a couple of weeks ago. I wanted to make my mark and I have. I felt it was important to come back here now. The new Labour government is supposed to be reviewing road building programmes. They are supposed to be the people's party so they should not be giving the taxpayers' money to big business to build roads."[11]

Not long afterwards the Government dropped most of the remaining road schemes they had inherited from the Tories and promised to boost public transport. Back at his former home in Hazlemere, High Wycombe, in Buckinghamshire, Swampy's mother Jill said adoringly, "I admire him very much for taking a stand. He feels strongly about things. He wants a nice environment for future generations." She admitted that her husband Peter, aged 54, was less enthusiastic about their son's activities. "My husband is a middle-aged man," said Mrs Hooper, "I think that sums it up. I've met very few men of his generation who would approve of what Daniel is doing."[12]

By August doubts were setting in as to Labour's intentions, and it was revealed that Environment and Transport supremo John Prescott had not one, but two gas-guzzling Jaguars in his garage. When a disillusioned nation needed him most, Swampy was suddenly no more. He handed back the £40,000 advance to Fourth Estate, abandoned a lucrative television contract and a daily newspaper column, and disappeared. His mother Jill told the *Sunday Times*, "The public attention was too much for him. He doesn't want to be a figurehead for the ecological movement or a media star. He wants to fade into the background and go back to being an ordinary person."[13]

Today Swampy lingers on in name only. A *Daily Telegraph* leading article may refer to someone as "the thinking person's Swampy", and the phrase "to do a Swampy" has become synonymous with the digging of tunnels. Though on the other side of the fence there has been a reaction from his fellow eco-warriors. "Don't use the S-word here," said one, "He's had too much exposure."

Swampy presumably agreed. He cut off his dreadlocks, asked people to call him plain Dan and went to live in Cornwall, doing voluntary work.

The Press missed him and in 1998 announced that it had found "the junior Swampy": an illiterate 11 year old eco-warrior known as General Survival. He was living with his mother in a tree house in woodland known as Silver Birches, next to the town hall in Epsom, Surrey. The General, Matthew Morris-Steward, and his mother, Lorraine Steward, were among 20 protesters occupying the wood to stop a road being built through it. Matthew had waist-length hair, dressed in a combat jacket and wore a general's hat. He said: "I am here because I want to save the Silver Birches and the wildlife on this site. I have friends who like the woodland because they can play in it. I like living in the tree house and spend my time picking up litter and tidying up the woods and parkland. Sometimes I help with the cooking. I like veggie food." He said the tree house was warm and cosy except when it rained. "I love it there mostly. All my friends come to play with me there and I don't want that to come to an end because the trees have all been chopped down to make a road. I want to save the trees for other children."[14]

Matthew had opted out of school at the age of eight. He said, "I was kicked out of The Mount school in Kingston because I was behind. I like my life now. I spend my days playing with former schoolfriends from Kingston, helping my mother find and prepare food and trying to learn how to read."

His mother said, "He believes in what we are doing. I just want to make the world a better place, more green and less concrete. I think we are a lot better off living in a tree house than on the council estate in Kingston where we used to live. That place was just a haven for drugs and crime." She and the other protesters claimed that Matthew, whose father died in 1990, had a right to stay in the tree house under Agenda 21 of the Rio Earth Summit agreement of 1992. Signed by Britain and 100 other countries, the agreement upheld the right of young people to come to the aid of their environment.

General Survival did very well for a while. With the help of publicist Max Clifford, Mrs Steward sold her son's story to the *News of the World* for a reported £10,000. Mr Clifford, whose previous clients have included such luminaries as OJ Simpson, said Matthew was "very cute and could be a new star". He said he had received inquiries from advertising agencies and American television stations who thought he might be "the next Macaulay Culkin" (child star of the hit movie *Home Alone*).

Alas, it was not to be. Back on the council estate, his former neighbours accused the General himself of being an environmental vandal. One elderly resident said, "If you know Matthew, he is anything but Green. I could write a book about that lot. They are the original neighbours from hell."

The *Daily Telegraph* investigated further and found that the three-bedroomed house where Matthew and his mother had lived before moving ("most of the time", as it now transpired) to the tree house, was "scruffy and the windows broken". More worryingly, "a 20ft pine tree in the back garden is dying because, neighbours said, Matthew and his brother, Luke, 13, had stripped it of all its branches." The paper also claimed the same pillar-box red paint used on the General's garden fence had been daubed on garden walls up and down the street. The *Daily Telegraph* quoted another resident as saying, "They are one disgusting family. When they're up a tree the rest of us love it, because they're not causing any damage here." The General's aunt, Sharon Morris-Latham, was particularly damning, "The whole thing is pathetic and makes me so angry. They only started getting involved with the tree protesters... after Lorraine got involved with one of them called Badger. Matthew doesn't have a clue about the environment and he is just being spoon-fed what to say. I just don't know how the media managed to get him looking so scrubbed-up in their pictures." On the rare occasions Matthew went to school, he was taken there and back by a council "'carer' in a minicab. One of his regular drivers told the *Daily Telegraph*, "He is the most foul-mouthed, belligerent, disobedient kid you will ever meet... and the mother is not too disimilar."[15] The authorities arranged special schooling for the General, Hollywood lost a star and the media its 'new Swampy'.

Swampy and General Survival illustrate the way the media functions in Britain. The news is extremely 'managed'. Stories and the characters who participate in them are very rapidly put in a narrowly defined slot. This is particularly so in tabloid journalism, where sub-editors pre-digest events and 'tailor' them for their readership: solidly middle class in the case of the *Daily Mail* and the *Daily Express*, working class in the case of the *Star* and the *Sun*, and with the hinterland between occupied by *The Mirror*. In the world of the 'red tops', where the audience is assumed to be not very bright, the sub-editor's job is to reduce everything to the simplest possible English using words of one, occasionally two syllables. The world that is created for readers is meant to be reassuring, thus encouraging them to continue purchasing the product. The papers create their own vocabulary ("hunk" + "stunna" = "bonk").

This peculiarly cut-off world has been slow to react to the advent of the eco-warrior and when forced to confront the species, has tended to resort to cliché rather than attempt to understand concerns or realistically report activities.

One of the most flagrant examples of this has come about in the reporting of the activities of the anarchist group Reclaim the Streets. Although RTS staged some of the most spectacular and imaginative anti-car protests of the 1990s, the general public knows remarkably little about them, as evidenced by media coverage. People are entitled to ask, as a bewildered cop investigating the activities of The Monkey Wrench Gang asks: "Who *are* these guys?"

RTS is not an underground movement. It is both visible and audible, referring to itself with some pride as another 'disorganisation', though it has offices, with phones, a fax machine and computers. Once again, for newspapers there is that slight problem of interpretation for a middle class readership, even though many RTS leading lights are highly literate. (They may take themselves just a tad too seriously for their own good but that is another matter). Activist John Jordan explains the movement's aims thus, "With the ecological crisis leading to what some have called a 'biological meltdown' and a social crisis that is demolishing what little local democracy or equality that exists, it seems that only radically creative and passionate strategies that bring into question every aspect of our industrialised society will avert catastrophe."[16]

Another RTS luminary, Paul Morozzo, says: "We are basically about taking back public space from the enclosed private arena. At its simplest it is an attack on cars as a principal agent of enclosure. It's about reclaiming the streets as public inclusive space from the private exclusive use of the car. But we believe in this as a broader principle, taking back those things which have been enclosed within capitalist circulation and returning them to collective use as a commons."[17]

The roots of Reclaim the Streets-type actions go back to 1971, when Victor Anderson – of the Young Liberal group Commitment

– organised an attempt to block Oxford Street in central London. *Peace News* hailed it as "the greatest street party London had ever seen" and said it was part of a campaign for free public transport and car-free streets. The paper said it was "a symbolic action against the car's domination of the city centre". Anderson said he had drawn inspiration from the radical peace movement The Committee of One Hundred – "We said there should be a Committee of One Hundred for the environment. It was quite clear that the car was the main problem and that streets were getting more congested."[18] Anderson organised a second street party in Picadilly Circus in 1973, but after that event the Reclaim the Streets idea lay dormant for two decades.

It was reborn during the M11 protests in Wanstead, but only really came into its own after a series of spectacular 'street parties' elsewhere in London that were unconnected with road building schemes. The first of these took place in Camden High Street, London, on a Saturday afternoon in May 1995. A staged car crash blocked the road; the drivers of the two cars involved climbed out and began shouting at one another. Then, as shoppers gawped in amazement, one of them started to smash the other's car with a hammer. RTS activists surged out of the crowd and jumped on top of the cars, continuing the wrecking process. They hurled paint over the road and unfurled a banner reading "RECLAIM THE STREETS – FREE THE CITY / KILL THE CAR". Around 500 people then emerged from a nearby Underground station and took over the street. They danced all afternoon to the Rinky Dink, a mobile bicycle-powered sound system. Trestle tables were set up in the middle of the road and free food was served. A climbing frame for children was erected at what, a short time before, had been a busy road junction.

This has gone down in RTS mythology as Street Party No.1. When night fell, people drifted away and eventually the police moved in and dispersed the protesters. John Jordan, who teaches Live Art at Sheffield Hallam University, claims the street party is an art form. "We were introducing play into politics, challenging the official culture's claims to authority, stability, sobriety, immutability and immortality by cheekily taking over a main traffic artery... The street party has no division between performer and audience, it is created by and for everyone, it avoids all mediation, it is experienced in the immediate moment by all, in a spirit of face-to-face subversive comradeship."[19]

Imagine trying to explain that to a *Sun* reader!

Street Party No.2, held two months later in Upper Street, Islington, in London attracted 3,000 people. This time roads were blocked using tripods. Banners were attached to lampposts, reading "CAR FREE", "STREET NOW OPEN" and – very simple and evocative – "BREATHE". Tons of sand were emptied onto the tarmac for children to play in and a band played folk music. An RTS flyer for the Upper Street party declared: "CARS CANNOT DANCE: When they move they are violent and brutish, they lack sensitivity and rhythm. CARS CANNOT PLAY: When they diverge from the straight and narrow, they kill. CARS CANNOT SOCIALISE: They privatise, separate, isolate and alienate."

What will probably go down in road protest history as Reclaim the Streets' finest hour came with Street Party No.3 in July 1996. An estimated 10,000 protesters took over the M41 motorway in London; dancing to a sound system, holding picnics in the central reservation, turning the fast lane into a sandpit for children, whilst entertainment was provided by fire eaters and jugglers. A scrap metal yard overlooking the motorway got involved by dangling a wrecked van from a crane and leaving it hanging high above the proceedings. One banner strung over the carriageway read, "THE SOCIETY THAT ABOLISHES EVERY ADVENTURE MAKES ITS OWN ABOLITION THE ONLY POSSIBLE ADVENTURE". Could the *Daily Mail* get to grips with that concept, do you think?

John Jordan recalls one of the most daring and symbolic acts of the event: "Some of the most striking images were the two huge carnival figures, 30 feet high with 10-feet-wide hooped skirts, with bagpipe players wearing Restoration wigs installed at the top of them. These seemingly innocent figures were wheeled up and down the motorway all day and night, but hidden under the skirts, away from the eyes of the police, and drowned out by the sound of techno, people were busy drilling into the tarmac with Kanga hammers and planting saplings rescued from the path of the M11 link road, which was still in the process of being built. The next morning, finding tarmac pockmarked with freshly planted saplings, the Highways Agency was forced to close the motorway for several days and resurface it."[20] Following this, police raided the RTS offices, impounded its computers and arrested an activist for conspiracy to cause criminal damage to a motorway.

The raid did not halt the anarchy for long. During the 1997 general election campaign that brought Tony Blair to power, RTS organised a poster campaign, "NEVER MIND THE BALLOTS... RECLAIM THE STREETS" and distributed spoof copies of the *Evening Standard*, proclaiming "GENERAL ELECTION CANCELLED". Then, during a two day 'Festival of Resistance' the movement organised a march of thousands of people into central London. Police managed to foil the original RTS plan to 'squat' the Department of the Environment but, as the march passed through Whitehall, they were unable to stop an activist climbing through an open window into the Foreign Office. The man made his way to an upper floor, opened another window and hurled hundreds of documents out of it onto the cheering crowd below. Jordan describes this as "an astoundingly filmic image, reminiscent of some archetypal revolutionary movie."[21] As the march passed Downing Street, red smoke bombs were thrown. Then, after a rally in Trafalgar Square, a street party was held in front of the National Gallery. Police baton-charged protesters at the other end of the square, and the *Sunday Express* was able to headline its story the following day, "RIOT FRENZY – ANARCHIST THUGS BRING TERROR TO LONDON". From the inside, John Jordan saw it somewhat differently of course. "It joined the celebratory spirit of a party with the rebellious release of a riot," he said. "It juxtaposed the living, thumping beat of a sound system with the cold classicism of the National Gallery." Or was Jordan merely trying to justify an action that for one reason or another was sadly lacking the vibrancy and imagination of the previous "street parties" and – let's face it – had very little to do with "reclaiming the streets"? Were RTS starting to lose the plot? Had the movement been hijacked by hardline anarchists for purely political ends? A great many people in the environmental movement – including some of their erstwhile supporters – say that this is the case.

The next major protest organised by RTS was a very different affair; far more political and confrontational. J18 was billed on the Internet as an "international carnival against capitalism" to be held in the square mile of the City of London, the capital's financial district, on June 18 1999. It was billed to coincide with the start of a G8 summit of the major industrialised nations in Cologne. Four thousand people heeded the call to protest against Third World debt, the arms trade and corporate greed in general. The event started peacefully enough. *The Times* reported: "Thousands of colourfully attired opponents of the global financial system banged drums and blew whistles outside the edifices of international capitalism. But the walls of Jericho failed to collapse and City traders responded in kind by pouring champagne on the protesters' heads and showering them with photocopied £50 notes. Some workers left their offices to join in the wild pagan dance being led around Liverpool Street to a military drum tattoo."[22]

Later in the day things turned nasty, however. Liffe, the international futures exchange, was stormed by 100 protesters. When traders repelled them and lowered a security grille, the activists smashed the glass doors of the exchange and trashed the reception area. They then smashed the glass walls of the nearby Rabobank building and wrecked offices inside. Reclaim the Streets' anti-car bias came to the fore in an attack on a Mercedes Benz dealership. The protesters set alight a Mercedes and a Daimler, and caused serious damage to a dozen other cars parked in the City. In one particularly ugly incident, a motorist was dragged from his car and bleach was poured over him. As police reinforcements arrived, two protesters were hit by police vans, one of them – a woman – was run over and trapped under a van. She was taken to hospital for the treatment of a broken leg and other injuries. By now, tempers were running high on both sides. In full 'Darth Vader' style riot gear, police charged the protesters and, under a shower of missiles, slowly drove them out of the City – but not before a water main had been set off and paint flung over the Bank of England. At least 30 people were injured and 16 arrests were made.

In seeking to explain this extraordinary happening to its readers, the *Sunday Times* resorted to that old chestnut from pre-Thatcher days of trade union confrontation – rent-a-mob. It's Insight team reported, "Police investigating the City of London riots are examining reports that some protesters were paid to attend the disturbances – the worst since the Trafalgar Square poll tax riots in 1990." The report continued, "...some protesters claimed they had been given £30, free transport and a packed lunch to travel to the event". The paper said the demo had turned into "an orgy of violence" and referred to demonstrators "fuelled by drink and drugs". The source of the rent-a-mob allegation was wisely buried in the 22nd paragraph of the story: "Some of the protesters said they had been paid to attend the event. Two claimed to be students from Nottingham University. They told traders at the Liffe exchange: 'We were asked if we wanted to come down to the protest. We were paid £30 each, given a free bus ride down and provided with a packed lunch.'"[23] Pretty slim, hearsay evidence from people with an axe to grind, you might think, but enough for the paper's leader writer to describe J18 as "the day that rent-a-mob came to the City of London".

Only the *Observer* made any real effort to explain the protest in an objective light. "Anne, who was 'criminalised' at the Newbury bypass, says the nature of environmental and class protest has changed, as a result of the continued defeats at specific sites around the country and bitterness at the timidity of the Labour Government. 'I was at Newbury, and we lost. I saw the land being trashed,' she says. 'A lot of us in the environmental movement are absolutely disenchanted with the old approach... There is no point fighting little battles across the country. We have to be more ambitious, and attack the system itself. That's why we targeted the City. Anyone who thinks and cares about the environment for long enough realises it is about the system, not individuals. What is the point of recycling bottles while BP, Shell and McDonald's rape the planet? We used to be fluffy. Now I won't condemn violence anymore. There are people who desperately want to change things. People voted for Labour and saw nothing changed. We are having to get tough to get heard." In a leading article the paper said: "The Green activism of the Seventies gave way to Green parliamentary candidates and environmentalists working with business to achieve change; with progress painfully slow and conventional politics huddling around the centre, the pendulum is swinging back to direct action. We can expect more protests like Friday's. We condemn the violence, but the wider truth stands. If you believe the earth is endangered by contemporary capitalism, things are getting worse, not better."[24]

There was widespread criticism of the police for not preventing the riots. There was good reason to suppose that after J18, in cooperation with M15, surveillance and infiltration of Reclaim the Streets rapidly became a priority. The next flashpoint came in December 1999 when in the so-called Battle of Seattle, the opening of a meeting of the World Trade Organisation was halted by a massive, well coordinated demonstration by a environmental activists. Protests also took place in London but were severely curtailed by police. There were violent clashes with Reclaim the Streets demonstrators at Euston station and a police van was set on fire. Seven people were injured and there were 38 arrests. Police said the demonstrators started the violence by throwing missiles at them. The protesters admitted this but said they had acted "out of pure frustration" because the police had not allowed them to express themselves. J18 had marked a radical departure from purely anti-car, environmental protest but had made political sense in that it was an attack on international capitalism, as the perceived cause of environmental destruction. Euston, however, was just an ugly, pointless mess. Where on earth, you wondered, would Reclaim the Streets be able to go from here?

11
THE NEXT ITEM ON THE AGENDA

The planned target for Reclaim the Streets' Mayday 2000 demonstration was the Millennium Dome. The giant 'new' Labour theme park in Greenwich was a symbol of all the disorganisation found repugnant in Tony Blair's 'Cool Britannia'. But RTS faced tremendous difficulties getting their show on the road. The Metropolitan Police, stung by criticism of its handling of J18, successfully – if rather heavy-handedly – contained Euston and was allowing RTS no rope. The group's activities have for some time been closely monitored by the security services. RTS also faces some difficult choices of its own if it is to survive and function as an effective pressure group. Those who have been with it from the start see a need for the 'disorganisation' to recover its 'soul' as an environmental, rather than extreme anarchist, movement. They also see a need for it to come to terms with the fact that the present spontaneous, uncontrolled nature of its protests allows many people who simply enjoy the prospect of a "bundle with the Bill", and care little about the environment or changing society to come along for the ride.

Even in sedate Cambridge, the RTS "street party" attracts a motley crowd. At the June 1999 event I caught the following snatch of conversation: "She's talking about saving the planet and all that bollocks and me, I'd like to just smash the whole bloody thing, blow it to pieces, you know what I mean?" Other protesters I talked to at the event, such as Jim, aged 33 and unemployed, appeared genuinely concerned. Jim carried a home-made placard that read "STOP THE ROT, CARS OR PLANET" and said: "I'm here for many reasons really. I want to stop the car taking over our society. I'm also concerned about its role in causing global warming and in the number of accidents it causes, a high proportion of them involving children. Then there's the manufacture of cars which involves very wasteful processes. Demonstrations like this are good because they get people to think about such things. It's all about taking control of your life, making yourself heard."[1]

Lee, aged 30, "a support housing officer working with the homeless", said he had no car, nor did he want one in the future. "There is a dreadful problem with traffic in this country. Something needs to be done. What we are doing here today is highlighting a problem that is nationwide, worldwide. If nothing is done, one day it will be gridlock, the whole damned thing will grind to a halt," he said. "But we're all here to have a good time too. The only violence you get at demonstrations like this is caused by the police. Of course, the motorists don't like it but it maybe starts them thinking a bit. And it triggers a debate afterwards in the pubs and in the local Press."[2]

A 26 year old girl wearing an elaborate hooped dress decorated with the cardboard centre pieces of hundreds of toilet rolls said she was "The Princess of Poo" and would grant me an audience. She said she was attending the demo because she was concerned about the environment. "Of course, I've come here to have some fun too but it's useful if it makes people who drive stop and think what they're doing to the planet and shows those that don't drive that they can make themselves heard. It's like an alternative method of lobbying, really. Nearly all the other channels of political protest have been exhausted as far as we are concerned. Everything is just so commercially oriented nowadays. There's no real interest in environmental issues. We're here to redress the balance. We want motorists to realise what they are doing to their country and the world they live in."[3]

On the other hand Steph, aged 23, from Ottawa, who was dressed and painted up as "some kinda fairy", said, "I'm just a tourist. I've been a couple of weeks in Cambridge and will soon be moving on. I'm just here for a laugh. I'm not at all concerned about the car. It's nice to dress up, that's all. There's demonstrations in Canada but nothing like this, nothing as colourful as this."

Colourful it certainly was. There were two cavaliers, one in yellow, the other in red, duelling with plastic swords; "Terry

Ping", who claimed to be (a very young looking) 78 and was dressed as a salesman in an outrageously loud jacket; an attractive dark-haired girl in a mini-skirt with a shiny blouson top emblazoned with the words "freak" and "sexual deviant"; a man in white pyjamas, open sandals and Mexican sombrero; and a punk wearing ripped tartan trousers and a 'Never Mind the Bollocks' T-shirt, which may not have been fancy dress at all, of course. Death added a sombre touch in his long black cape, carrying a sickle. Someone – obviously a Swedish film buff – called to him, "Fancy a game of chess?"

Around 300 people eventually turned up at the rendezvous in front of Cambridge railway station. Oblivious to the steadily falling rain, we marched – perhaps 'drifted' would be a better word – through the city streets causing mild traffic havoc, though all the time being closely monitored by police. Where we were going, no one knew. We were told simply to follow the music, provided by a trombonist and two saxophonists. There were some fairy tale moments: three young girls wearing long, flowing dresses dancing in front of stranded cars, holding hands in the summer rain; marchers calling to drivers with families aboard, "Free your children!"; and the cavaliers shouting to women passengers, "Leave your husbands!" One driver got his own back by shouting at protesters who were smoking, "Put out your cigarettes and save the Earth!"

There were also a few nasty moments. When the police impounded the RTS sound system in the car park of a local nursery school, demonstrators surrounded the building, disrupting a fund-raising fete that was going on inside and frightening children and their parents. Thelma Rumball, head of the nursery, said later, "It was absolutely terrifying for us. We didn't know what was going on."[4] With the sound system abandoned, the march wound its wet way to the site for the street party at the bottom of Mill Road, where two cars accelerated towards protesters, only narrowly missing them. The march was joined by a man who normally spent his days on a seat in St Barnabas churchyard, swigging lager and calling to passers-by for change. Eyes shining dementedly, he ran along a line of halted cars beating on their roofs. I had never seen him so animated. In the jargon of the day, I suppose you could say he had been temporarily empowered.

The rain was by now pouring relentlessly down but the demonstrators hung bunting from lampposts, slung "STOP THE CAR" banners between trees, sat in the road and held their party anyway; drowning any sorrows they might have had in cans of lager purchased from the local off licence. One of the last images I had of the party was of a man in a blonde wig wearing a long dress and swigging from a bottle of champagne. He was weaving around uncertainly in front of the police lines, kicking at empty lager cans with his hob-nailed boots. I walked home, dripping wet, down a wonderfully quiet street and learned next day that there had been 14 arrests when police later broke up the party: one man was charged with supplying a class B drug, two others were cautioned for being drunk and disorderly and the other 11 were all freed with no action taken.

In an attempt to take the current pulse of Reclaim the Streets, I telephoned the RTS office in London and was told that I would be welcome to go to one of their meetings. Indeed, when I said I was writing a book about the fight against the car, the chap who answered the phone actually promised to put me "on the agenda". Thus it was that on a dark winter's night, I made my way to the Arsenal Tavern in Blackstock Road, Finsbury Park, North London.

Here, in the back room, RTS was holding a meeting. I arrived to find a diverse, largely male crowd of about 50 people assembled, most of them in their mid 20s to early 30s. There were several shaven heads, some dreadlocks but also some devastatingly conventional hair cuts, similarly a few earrings and lip-studs but a great many unpierced, quite ordinary faces. The dominant dress was jeans or combats, worn with T-shirts, one bearing the less-than-revolutionary slogan 'Echo and the Bunnymen'. Some of those present sported coarse woven jackets of the type sold in 'fair trade' shops, others bulky fishermen's sweaters. There were around half a dozen women who wore jeans and chunky sweaters. There was an older man who reminded me of Dexter Gordon (a tenor saxophonist), quite stylish in a dark suit and black Jim Perry shirt.

The meeting began with a ceremonial shifting of chairs to form a large circle. Then we all sat looking around expectantly. To my right was a man obviously in gainful employment (I heard him tell his friend he was thinking of donating a percentage of his wages to RTS). To my left was a hawk-nosed, very bitter looking, conventionally clad individual with black Brylcremed hair. He kept looking about him defiantly and muttering furiously to himself.

Someone deposited papers in the centre of the circle and, feeling rather self-conscious, I left my seat and picked up a selection. One was quite amusing. It read: "Unfortunately, due to the influx of parasitic elements we have been forced to introduce an entrance exam. Full marks are expected. 1. What year was the Kronstadt uprising? 2. Most, Goldman, Kropotkin, Bakunin. Which of these didn't have a silly beard? 3. Who wrote *The Dispossessed*? 4. Cartoon hedgehogs were prominent in the publications of which revolutionary group? 5. If S is surplus value, K is constant capital and V is variable capital (labour), give the formula for the rate of profit."

Having scored one out of five, I passed rapidly on to another paper. This was composed by one Albert Parsons and entitled *'FreeDome' a few ideas*. The first idea was as follows: "Imagine 50,000 leaflets distributed around the country. Perfect full colour spoofs of the Millennium dome leaflet, bright yellow with 'An amazing Day... Mayday 2000. Free entry to the dome' splashed across the front. On the back in New Labour double speak, the text explains that by presenting the leaflet at the dome you get free entrance on May 1st 2000... It then goes on to explain that New Labour have realised that the dome does after all belong to the people and that perhaps it should not be just a corporate circus and temple to capitalism." And so on. At one juncture in what rapidly became a stream-of-political-consciousness rant, Mr Parsons made the perfectly valid point that "the media have focused on the confrontational aspect of RTS, the positive celebration of alternatives that the street party heralded has been lost in the spectacle of riot, chaos and anarchy." He said "the key is openness and communication", before urging his readers "to grasp the moment".

The 'gender sub-group' were being neither open nor communicative. A terse announcement for their meeting at the Spiral Squat, 402 Queensbridge Road, Dalston, said it was for "women only".

As I digested these and other pieces of information, a "facilitator" was chosen to lead the meeting and make sure everyone who wanted to could have his – or her – say. The "facilitator" was Simon; shaven-headed and fiery-eyed in camouflage combats and a bright orange T-shirt, who struck an heroic pose, left hand on hip, as with his right he held out the minutes of the last meeting which were duly distributed. These were not called 'minutes', of course, but "some points... not in any particular order" and finished up with the words, "That's all I can remember and it's all approximate." They too were concerned with Mayday 2000 and promised, among other things, "If it's good, it's going to be creative as fuck. Time to invoke the collective Situationist genius." Point No. 8 read, "Involvement of a broad range of groups and sectors of society is in many ways A Good Thing. This would be easier for an open action." This was interesting in view of what happened next.

We were all asked to call out our names and a rather harassed looking chap with curly hair seated near Dexter Gordon announced that he was Charlie, a member of the Socialist Workers' Party and a journalist for *Socialist Worker*. This was greeted with cries of derision, one of them from the Brylcreme-coiffeured man to my left. The small female contingent, gathered in one corner, was particularly vocal in expressing its dislike of the SWP. One of its members said she was of the candid opinion that you could not work with SWP members because they hijacked every cause they got involved in for their own ends. Charlie pleaded, "Look, I was invited to come here. Couldn't we try to find some common ground?"

The chap sitting next to Charlie confessed that he too was a member of the SWP – not only that but he was Scottish. He pointed out that May Day was a traditional working class festival, and a time to demonstrate solidarity. At this point, someone whose name (I think) was "Sudge" pointed out that it was also an important date in the pagan calendar. This caused great consternation. The Brylcremed man to my left fidgeted violently and snapped, "Not for me it ain't, mate."

A man who described himself as a campaigner for animal rights said that he did not really understand what was going on, whereupon someone assured him good naturedly that no one else did either: "We don't know what we are doing – that's how we keep it a secret," said somebody else and everyone laughed. The meeting then returned to more serious matters. It was stated that there should be no compromise with NGOs (Non Governmental Organisations), to which some poor chap cried in anguish, "Hey, aren't we an NGO?"

The soul-searching continued. Various participants admitted to being members of the Anarchist Federation, including both Dexter Gordon and the Brylcremed man to my left. There were also representatives of a group called People's Global Action present. For a brief, strange moment I fully expected someone to own up to being there on behalf of MI5.

During all of this I noted a strange, slightly sinister habit of RTS regulars: a ritualistic brandishing of both arms in front of them with fingers twitching when they either disagreed or were bored with what someone was saying. At least that was my interpretation, perhaps there was a deeper significance (the warding off of revisionist evil?).

The proceedings were permeated by the noise of a pinball machine in the next room and, until someone went out for a chat with the landlady, occasional bursts of loud rock music from a speaker at the back of the room. It all ended for me when everyone divided into sub-groups to plot Mayday 2000. I explained that I did not wish to participate in this, but merely wanted to talk to someone about RTS for a book I was writing. I was confronted by a veritable forest of twitching arms coupled with derisory catcalls from the female contingent – one of whom, I remember, made a rather cutting remark concerning my age. They told me that I should wait until the meeting was over, to which I replied that I would not have time for that as I had to get the train – the train, mark you – back to Cambridge. But of course plotting the downfall of international capitalism came first. I had long ago realised that I was not on the agenda, because there wasn't one. There was only one thing to do. I grasped the moment and left, just in time to get the 21.51 from King's Cross.

Back in the real world, having coined the aphorism, "Never trust a man who can tell you the date of the Kronstadt uprising", I went looking for an antidote to RTS. I wanted to meet people who could offer a radical and imaginative alternative to a society dominated by the car, yet were not burdened by the arcane ideology of anarchy. And lo, it came to pass that I found Andy Castellano Smith and Tom Williams, furiously pedalling their way to a better, less polluted future. Andy and Tom are members of Critical Mass, a "celebration of cycling and a demonstration of the alternative it offers to fuming traffic congestion" – in a word, or rather three: bicycling en masse.

Critical Mass started life in San Francisco when, as Andy puts it, "six or seven years ago a group of bicycle couriers got fed up with traffic and decided that on Friday nights they would ride home together from work." They attracted other cyclists, and then someone came up with the idea of a mass ride around the city to protest against the dominance of cars. This became a regular event and proved enormously popular. The idea spread to England soon afterwards, and today the Critical Mass ride through central London is a regular event. Held on the last Friday of every month, with its starting point on the south bank of Waterloo Bridge at 6pm, the ride attracts up to 1,500 riders on summer evenings. There is a hard core of 100-200 dedicated cyclists, including Andy and Tom, who take part throughout the year. It mightily annoys some drivers, and in the beginning there was "the odd problem with the police" but Andy says this was soon sorted out. "The thing is," he said, "there is nothing illegal about it, so long as no one organises it."

So, of course, no one does. "We get all sorts of people on the ride," says Andy, "I think each person has a different reason for being there. But of course it's a way of pointing out that there are far too many cars on the road and a lot of people are angry at the lack of consideration given to cyclists on the road. Traffic planning is nearly always aimed at helping the flow of cars and only rarely takes account of cycling, which is an environmentally friendly way of getting about."

Andy, aged 30, practised what he preached. Each day he cycled from his home in Walthamstow to Guys Hospital where he worked as a computational imager. "It's eight and a half miles. I quite like it, despite the pollution. I think London is better than a lot of other cities when it comes to bikes. It's far quicker than it would be going by car, because of the congestion. But it is a bit of a daily struggle with all the traffic and once I got knocked off my bike when someone opened a car door in front of me." He does have a car himself, although it has been off the road for two years. He drove to work only twice before giving up: "It took two hours. It takes 35 minutes by bike." Tom, 27, an access officer with Ealing Council, who also has a car, will not use it to get to work either: "It takes one hour, forty minutes to get there by car, an hour by bike."

Critical Mass has staged mass bike rides to coincide with some Reclaim the Streets demos, including J18, but Tom – "I'm involved with the Labour Party" – was anxious to distance the movement from them. "We're not anarchists," he said. I told him I was mightily relieved to hear it. "We don't have any special political philosophy. We just want the right to cycle safely and point out that there is an alternative to the car. We work within the system. We lobby. Why, we once got 100 MPs out on a mass bike ride. We even have off-duty policemen riding with us." Tom is passionate about his biking: "I've always been mad keen on it. My parents claim I could cycle before I could walk."

He says the Critical Mass rides have become a major social event for many people. "We even have our own four-wheeled mobile sound system. The tourists love it. The Japanese take pictures of us."

In addition to the ride through central London, a Critical Mass ride also happened (the preferred terminology) in Richmond Park, on the first Sunday in the month during the summer 1999. This was a protest against cars being allowed through the park at weekends, when families are out walking or picnicking. "The speed limit is 30 miles an hour, which is ridiculously high considering the circumstances," said Andy. "I mean, you've got kids playing there – and deer are regularly killed by cars. They close Parliament Hill on Sundays, why not Richmond Park?"

Tom believes that other European countries have more enlightened transport policies than those in Britain. The reason for this is that they have at one time or another been social democracies, and as a result their societies are more homogenous, with less confrontation between different interest groups. "Britain is in a very bad state when it comes to transport. The Government knows what it's got to do but it's afraid to act. Personally I think civil servants are to blame for a great deal of the inactivity. They just want things to stay the same so they frighten MPs into doing nothing. And the media in this country makes no effort to lead or educate the public. As for all this stuff about squeezing the motorist, well motorists are also pedestrians – they know there's a problem and they'd probably be a lot more sympathetic to measures against cars than people give them credit for."

Critical Mass also offer support for the families of cyclists killed on the roads. "We gather at the spot, lay flowers and light candles, stop the traffic for a while," explained Andy. "We show the relatives of the deceased that someone really cares."

"What has happened in this society," said Tom, "is that the motor car has become an acceptable way to kill people."

Critical Mass is also campaigning for the right to take bicycles on trains. "Bicycles should be treated as luggage," says Tom. "On rush-hour trains there should be a special carriage for bikes. Cyclists are fare paying passengers the same as everyone else."

Both Tom and Andy said that while many motorists did get angry when confronted with Critical Mass rides, violence was rare. "Only one person has ever been arrested on one of our rides and the police later dropped charges." One of the nastiest incidents involved a severely drunken pedestrian who took it into his head to halt a ride.

For his holidays Andy went to San Francisco, so he could ride with Critical Mass in the place where the movement was born. "It was very different," he said. "I found the police far more threatening than in London."

The Critical Mass rides have become a fact of life in many British cities. A report from Birmingham to the CM website admitted that "one or two hot heads" attracted police attention "by performing kamikaze stunts in the middle of dual carriageways." As a result, motor-cycle police accompanied the cyclists for a few rides. "They made no attempt to stop us and helped us get around difficult junctions, although they did clamp down on red light jumping, cyclists without lights etc. There was a period when they tried to get Friends of the Earth to take responsibility for the rides and register them as an official demonstration, but dropped the idea when they realised that CM is not organised by FoE or any other group and is simply a spontaneous and coincidental assertion of cyclists (to their) right to use the road." [5]

While I still do not know the date of the Kronstadt revolution, I have learned a great deal in the process of writing this book and I wish it to be known that if ever there should be a mass bike ride over that ****** sliproad to the A14 in Cambridge, or round and round the ******* ghastly, fume-filled roundabout that precedes it, thus causing a traffic jam that stretches to Felixstowe and back, then yours truly had nothing whatsoever to do with organising it.

It just happened

AN ALTERNATIVE DAY AFTER TOMORROW

In a year sometime in the third millennium, on a summer Sunday, a family in a town somewhere set out on a journey. They left their Home Zone, with its trees and tubs of flowers, birds singing and children playing happily in the street and, carrying their lightweight fold-up bicycles, took an electric shuttle bus into town. They debited their travel cards in the bus's automatic scanning machine, placed their bikes in the copious luggage rack and sat down. As they travelled the two adults watched the news on their wrist-TVs. The main item concerned Prince Harry, who had become an astronaut and was due to blast off on his first mission, after spending time with other astronauts relaxing in the Hilton Orbiter space hotel. Scientists then explained the new space-time reactive propulsion system that it was hoped would allow us finally to leave the solar system and journey to other star systems.[1]

Then there was an item on the filling-in of the cut through Twyford Down, and the efforts that were being made to faithfully restore it to the way it had been in the time of the legendary Dongas, who, as everyone knew, had helped lay the foundations for a new and better world. There were pictures of volunteers replanting rain forests in Asia and South America. Others included the work that was being done by the World Federation's environmental agency, working with the space programme, to replenish the ozone layer in the earth's upper atmosphere.

The news reader announced that the population of South America was at long last falling; it was hoped that poverty there would soon be abolished as it had been elsewhere in the world. He pointed out that the situation in South America was similar to the one that had existed at the turn of the century in China and India, but which had been reversed thanks to the famous "one child is enough" scheme in which traditional, misguided attitudes had been overcome. The news reader explained that Britain's pioneer programme of birth control and the resulting reduction of population had made possible the demolition of the old housing estates, and for landscaped parks to take their place. The next, related, item concerned Birmingham which, following massive reconstruction, had just been voted Most Beautiful City in Europe. Finally there were pictures from Antarctica, which had been declared a World Park in which no development of any kind would ever be permitted.

The children cycled to school each day down special bike lanes that were segregated from the road. The little boy took part in thrilling interactive CD-video programmes about the World Parks in Africa and India, where lions and tigers had been saved from extinction. The little girl and her friends 'travelled' under the sea with dolphins and whales in the school simulation unit. In the evenings, after they had eaten, the family would join their neighbours in the Home Zone; the parents sitting chatting with friends as the kids played happily together.

The bus eventually deposited the family at the monorail station, where they were taking a train to one of the national parks. The boy stared at a strange shiny metal object set in concrete on the forecourt of the station. "What's that, daddy?" he asked.

"That's a car," said his father, "It's there to remind us of how stupid we used to be." He smiled sadly. "There were lots of them when I was young. They were very dangerous things and they caused serious problems but we didn't know any better then. The route the monorail runs on used to be a motorway."

"A what?"

"A motorway. A very big road, crowded with cars and lorries."

"But lorries just go from the station to the shops."

"They do now. Then they used to go all over the country. Motorways were very dangerous. There used to be the most awful crashes."

"Then why did they have them?" asked his son.

His father sighed. "It was the way we got to places. To go out like we are now, we would have to travel in one of those pieces of metal and it used to take far longer to get where we're going because the roads were full of other people all doing the same thing."

The little boy stared at the monument and scratched his head.

Their train arrived and – along with a great many other families – they boarded the monorail. The train slid silently out of the station, through the city with its parks and Home Zones, past the John Tyme memorial and out into the countryside. The sun shone on the forests and the lakes.

The father remembered how ugly it all was when he was a boy. He remembered the industrial wastelands and the featureless streets of brick houses that had existed before the Home Zones, streets filled with cars, where no children could play because of the risk of accidents. "My God," he thought, "How things have changed!"

There are a few, blissful places in the present day world where the car's domination of society has already been ended; where people come first. These are called Home Zones. Home Zones have been in Europe for around 30 years and are at long last being introduced in socially backward Britain. In a street inside a European Home Zone, pedestrians have the right of way and the speed limit for cars is reduced to walking pace. Veteran anti-car campaigner Wolfgang Zuckermann explains the planning principles: "Street space should primarily be laid out for slow traffic. Conditions should be optimal for walking, playing, shopping, and so on. The motorist is only a guest."[2] Linda Beard, who runs the Streets for People campaign for the environmental pressure group Transport 2000, and which led the drive for British Home Zones, said, "I suppose the easiest way to explain it is that the street becomes one big zebra crossing. Of course we are talking about residential streets and ones in which most cars would belong to people living in the area anyway."[3]

The Home Zone revolution started in a residential area of the Dutch city of Delft in the 1960s, after three children had been killed there in road accidents. When the authorities refused to take action, the residents took the law into their own hands. One night they dug up and reconstructed their street, greatly restricting it to traffic and making it a place where their children could play in safety. They called this a woonerf, or "living yard".

It was totally illegal of course, but when local council officials arrived with police and bulldozers to undo their work, the residents defied them, attracting considerable media coverage. The forces of law and order retreated, and in 1976 woonerfs were not only given legal status but made a part of official Dutch planning policy. To qualify for conversion to a woonerf, it was decided, a street should not be a through traffic route, likely to be used by trucks or large buses – neither should it have a traffic flow of more than 100 vehicles an hour.

As Dutch is not one of the world's most easily assimilable languages, woonerfs rapidly became known elsewhere as Home Zones. There are now more than 6,500 in Holland and others in Germany, Austria, Denmark and Sweden, with nine scheduled for Britain. Linda Beard admits there has been considerable opposition in the UK: "The onus in this country has always been on pedestrians and cyclists to make sure they are safe. We want to change that so that the onus is on car drivers. They won't like it but it's something they are just going to have to get used to. The trouble is the media in this country seems to enjoy confrontation and often stirs up quite unnecessary controversy."[4]

Lynn Sloman, Transport 2000's assistant director, who helped to organise a trip to Holland for British community groups interested in establishing Home Zones, said the zones they visited were friendly places. "We spoke to residents eating breakfast together at a giant table in the middle of one street in Utrecht. In Home Zones in Utrecht and Delft, we heard from residents how elderly people felt much less isolated than they would do in an ordinary street." In Rijswijk, local resident Ivar Nijhuis told her, "I like living here because it's safe for the children to play in the street. There's also a little playground at the end of the street where they can go and play on their own. There are quite a lot of families around here and I know people will look out for them."[5]

Sloman said British traffic engineers on the trip could see no reason why the Dutch experience should not be replicated in Britain. "Some of the basic design ideas are very easy to copy," she said. "For example, cars in a Dutch Home Zone are often parked at right-angles to the road, leaving only a narrow space for traffic to get past. There is no separate pavement: the whole space is designed to be shared by pedestrians, cyclists and drivers. There are slides and rocking horses in the street, with benches, tables and chairs, plus trees and flower tubs. Car speeds are very low, partly because the design of the road makes it difficult to drive at more than a few miles an hour, but also because the law is clear that motorists must travel at no more than a walking pace. The sign at the entrance to the Home Zone tells drivers that they do not have priority."[6]

In a new development at Strijp, near Rijswijk, residents were consulted on the design of their Home Zone. One of them told Sloman, "Before a single brick was laid, a committee of future residents met with the developers to discuss the design and make changes." Sloman said this was the most important lesson of the tour: "For Home Zones to work in Britain, they have to be designed by community groups and local councils working together, not imposed on residents from above."[7]

Of the nine pilot Home Zones to be given approval by the government, one of the first to be up and running will be in the Methleys, a cluster of back-to-back Victorian terraced houses in Chapel Allerton, Leeds. The Methleys hit the headlines in 1996 when, in a dramatic protest against cars, residents turfed over the tarmac in one street for a weekend and held a party. Among the novel features of its Home Zone will be a "screen on the wall" open-air cinema at the end of one row of houses. In common with other zones, there will also be more greenery, flowers, trees and play areas for children, with traffic speeds greatly reduced – albeit only voluntarily in the beginning. People living in the area already drive at a self-imposed 10mph. Now members of the Methleys Neighbourhood Action group have helped to successfully lobby MPs for a change in the law, in order to allow local authorities to reduce speed limits without government approval. Schoolgirl Siobhan Hodson, one of the members of the group, travelled with Action 2000 to Holland. She talked to young people there who told her how Home Zones had changed their lives. She said, "I've got three younger brothers and a little sister and they can't really play out because of the cars, and we have only a tiny garden. I'd like to see a big communal garden and trees coming out into the road so cars have to go very slow to go around them. It would be nice to have somewhere that children can play and cars aren't allowed at all."[8] Not surprisingly, it was the play areas in the Dutch Home Zones that impressed her most. "Swings and slides in the street: they were brilliant! There were kids everywhere playing on them," she said.[9]

Others on the trip were equally impressed. Martin Hemmenway, of North Yorkshire Police, made the point that Home Zones reduce opportunities for criminals. "The more people there are, walking and cycling, sitting and playing, the less there will be a problem with crime," he said. "Home Zones make sense from many angles: traffic safety, community safety and personal safety." Margaret Trimble, of the Wolverhampton Limes Road Residents' Committee, said, "The Home Zones we saw were wonderful: clean, quiet and friendly. The atmosphere made me realise what we've lost in England." And Jennie Maybury, a Nottingham City Council planner, said, "Home Zones made the street space available to everybody. It was almost like taking the inside outside: extending the living space into the street."[10]

Another of the nine pilot Home Zones is to be in Ealing, West London. To celebrate being selected for the honour, the Five Roads Forum which had campaigned for the zone, persuaded the council to close off a road for a day, so that they could have some idea of what life in a future zone would be like. Residents brought sofas, rugs and pot plants outside, the local Waitrose supermarket provided champagne and Roads Minister Lord Whitty arrived to toast the success of the scheme.

Other Home Zones will be created in Lambeth, South London; Northmoor in Manchester; Magor Village in Monmouthshire; Nobel Road, Nottingham; New England in Peterborough; Morice Town, Plymouth; and Cavel Way in Sittingbourne, Kent. They will not, however, quite measure up to their European counterparts: the speed limit will not be lowered below 20mph and cars will still have priority. Transport 2000 continues to press for a 10mph speed limit and a change of priority to favour pedestrians.

On the one and only visit I ever made to Scotland, I have to confess it crossed my mind that climate change there might actually be beneficial, but of course the locals do not see it that way. Lothian Regional Council has been looking at innovative ways of drastically cutting pollution levels and car dependency. Its "moving forward" transport policy has seen the introduction of a new express bus way from Edinburgh city centre to the western suburbs, the airport and West Lothian, interchanging with trains at a new station, Edinburgh Park. David Begg, chairman of the Lothian Regional Council's transportation committee, says, "There is presently a vicious circle of ever increasing dependence on the car, caused by concentrating investment on motorists' needs. We hope to reverse that by judging transport investments principally on their contribution to improving road safety and reducing car use." The council is also experimenting with what it calls "car free areas", estates for people without cars, special buses for the disabled, city-wide provision of safe cycle lanes and "safe routes to school". The council is also encouraging the oldest means of transport: walking. Begg believes it is good for business: "Walking benefits shops in Edinburgh and Lothian. Window displays will only reach their target audience if that audience is on foot. There is strong international evidence that high quality pedestrian facilities in city centres and local shopping areas lead to increased retail turnover, directly benefiting local business and maintaining employment in the retail sector."[11]

Elsewhere in Britain, Manchester and Sheffield have successfully reintroduced modernised versions of the tram, which more accurately should be known as "light railways". Manchester's Metrolink, launched in 1992, runs on a combination of on-street city centre tramlines and converted suburban train tracks. It has been a huge success, used by more than 14 million people a year, and it is claimed that car traffic has dropped by 10 percent in the areas it serves. One of the disadvantages of light railways is that start-up costs are high: in the case of Manchester £145 million. Because of this, the Government has rejected a light railway scheme for Liverpool and stalled approval on other schemes in Leeds and Portsmouth, telling these cities they should provide more buses instead. The Sheffield Supertram was poorly planned and got off to a quite disastrous start in 1994 but demand rose at the rate of 13 percent a year and it was hoped the service would break even by 2001.

In rural Wiltshire, there have been experiments with a 'wiggly' bus that has no fixed route and can be 'hailed' by telephone. Kate Freeman, of the Pewsey Vale Transport Appraisal Group, said, "We want to get as near the convenience of the motor car as possible. It will be a bit like calling a cab but at a fraction of the cost, and we will make sure the service is comfortable, safe and reliable." The standard fare would be £1.[12]

It may not be long before someone comes up with a modern version of the trolleybus. These ran on tyred wheels but made use of overhead powerlines. The result was a remarkably smooth and efficient ride. In 1950 a spokesman for the British Electrical and Allied Manufacturers Association, was asked to answer this question, "Why should I care whether I ride on a trolleybus or a motor bus?" He replied, "From your question, madam, it rather looks as if you have not experienced riding in a trolley bus. You will find that the trolleybus is a vehicle which has a considerably greater capacity so that you will stand for a shorter time in the queue. You will be able to read your paper or do your crossword in complete comfort since the trolleybus gives very smooth riding. No, madam, you really don't know what bus comfort is until you have travelled by trolleybus." However, when they were phased out a decade later, a spokesman for London Transport said, "The public never really took to them – they were efficient but characterless... Lack of enthusiasm in trolleybuses is probably because they are efficient. The Londoner has never complained about them, so I suppose he has nothing to be sentimental about when they go."[13]

Car sharing has never really got off the ground, either in Britain or Europe. This is probably because a car is most often seen by its owner as a very personal possession; almost an extension of his or her self, not something to be shared, although one modern car is very much like any other. Hence the bewildering spectacle of thousands of metal boxes on wheels most of them containing just one person edging painfully slowly towards city centre destinations each day.

As for cycling, even its adherents admit there are problems. David Henshaw, who edits the cycling magazine A to B, from his home in West Park, Castle Cary in Somerset, says: "It's hard to see how significant numbers can be encouraged to cycle without a major and sustained investment to make cycling safer, by controlling cars."

He would like to see 20mph limits in all urban areas, 40mph on country roads, obligatory speed limiters on car engines, and increased road vehicle fuel taxation, plus substantial spending on public transport. Henshaw, who is also a great rail enthusiast, says buses have a great role to play but are no substitute for proper investment. "Just look at London's Oxford Street – it's car-free, but it's as polluted and congested as ever. That problem is echoed on a smaller scale in the centre of most cities – trams are the only civilised alternative. And 'heavy rail' for longer distances, of course." Here he condemns British rail privatisation as "a disaster" and says, "It has achieved nothing beyond holding back investment for five, ten or more years. And the new emphasis on market forces is doing little to reduce road traffic growth – in some areas it's actually having the opposite effect. Stations are no longer proposed in urban areas, where they'd be accessible to pedestrians and cyclists – most proposals are for motorway/parkway stations." Mainland Europe has long been way ahead of England when it comes to public transport; trains, buses and trams are clean, efficient and comfortable. For longer journeys, high-speed trains provide an economic and far more comfortable alternative to travel by car. Thanks largely to Mrs Thatcher's anti-rail phobia, Britain has nothing that can compare.

David Henshaw sees a great future for folding and electric bicycles. "Without government action, we have to act on a personal level. Good quality folding bikes can be very effective in combination with buses and trains, providing seamless door-to-door journeys. Electric bikes are potent weapons in the battle against the sort of short-haul car journeys that make absolutely no sense. Folding bikes will get smaller and lighter with improved reliability. Electric bikes will get lighter with improved range. Panasonic have introduced a viable folding bike weighing less than 7kg in Japan and I'd predict an electric bike with an 80km range within a year or so. If we are going to bring significant numbers of people over to cycling we have to accept new ideas and new technologies."[14]

Europe also leads the way when it comes to curbing the car. When I first went to Sweden, I was somewhat taken aback while out driving one day to encounter a new road sign. It read *Fart hinder*, giving me one of the rare laughs I had in that austere country. The smile was soon, quite literally knocked off my face. With a violent jolt, the car reared over a sudden obstacle in the road and came crashing down the other side, doing neither it nor me very much good. This was my first encounter with what are now commonly known as "sleeping policemen" (though I still prefer to think of them as *fart hinders*).[15]

Nowadays, they are just one of many devices used in what the planners call "traffic calming", designed to persuade motorists to slow down. Others include chicanes, rumble strips, and traffic throttles. Wolfgang Zuckermann says, "Up to now traffic engineers had automatically thought that the solution to better traffic movement was to make a road wider with fewer obstacles. Traffic calming reversed that approach in suggesting the opposite, to make a road narrower with more obstacles."[16]

His native Germany has taken the lead in Europe by adopting traffic calming measures in many major cities. David Engwicht, of the Australian pressure group, Citizens Advocating Responsible Transport (CART), recalls a visit to Nuremberg: "On my trip I walked across a bridge which once carried 30,000 vehicles. Now up to 25,000 pedestrians use it every hour. Approaching this bridge I joined a crowd listening to some musicians. On the bridge itself were brightly coloured market stalls. On the other side I was drawn into a side street by the laughter and shrieks of children. A little further up the street a number of people stood around a dramatic sculpture and fountain... This roadway, which once roared with the sound of 30,000 vehicles now resounded with the sound of children, laughter, music, chatter, and the soothing murmur of water. A planner showing me around Nuremberg indicated a street which had just been converted to a mixed use... with a 20 km/h speed limit. Pointing to a sidewalk cafe surrounded by planter boxes of vibrant flowers and people chatting under brightly coloured umbrellas, he said: 'See that? A year ago none of that was there. It is only after we calmed the traffic that the people and the flowers appeared. It was only then the people felt they could come out and enjoy their street again.'"[17]

The need to reclaim not just the streets, but our whole society from the car has never been more apparent. A quite horrendous example of the alienation it has created was revealed just one week into the third millennium. The badly decomposed body of an elderly woman was found on the central reservation of the Stafford Street ring road through Wolverhampton. It was that of Kathleen Childerley, who had walked out of a residential nursing home elsewhere in the city in May 1996 and had never been seen again. Kathleen, who was 65 years old and most likely in a depressed state of mind at the time, somehow contrived to stumble into the brambles and bushes on the reservation, and died there. Her body, discovered when contractors arrived to widen the road, had lain in the middle of a bustling city, with millions of motorists driving past, for three and a half years.[18]

All the indications are that things will get even worse if action is not taken. John Adams, Professor of Geography at University College, London, in a study commissioned for the Organisation for Economic Co-operation and Development (OECD), has warned that we are heading towards a state of what he describes as "hypermobility"; a trend of travelling further and faster every day which will undermine community life. Adams says the IT revolution is likely to accelerate this trend. The use of computers, while they may eliminate many journeys because work and some shopping can be done from home, will liberate workers "to join the exodus to the suburbs, and beyond, where most journeys – to shop, to school, to doctor, to library, to post office and to friends are all longer, and mostly infeasible by public transport." According to Adams, the more social and business contacts we make in cyberspace, the greater our need for real face-to-face encounters. "Transport and communications provide the means by which everyone connects with everyone else in the world. The transformation – historical and projected – in the speed and reach of these means is having profound social consequences."

Adams says there is a danger in placing too much trust in technology. "There are limits to what technology can do. A constraint on our behaviour that technology cannot relax is the number of hours in a day. As we spread ourselves ever wider, we must spread ourselves thinner. If we spend more time interacting with people at a distance, we must spend less time with those closer to home and if we have contact with more people we must devote less time and attention to each one. In small scale pedestrian societies – hypomobile societies – everyone knows everyone. In hypermobile societies old-fashioned geographical communities are replaced by aspatial communities of interest – we spend more of our time, physically, in the midst of strangers. The advantages of mobility are heavily advertised; the disadvantages of hypermobility receive much less attention."[19]

Ben Plowden, of the Pedestrians Association, commenting on Adams' report, said it confirmed that Britons were retreating from their communities by trying to cram too much into their working days. He said, "There is this growing devotion to travelling further, faster every day – but is that progress? The longer we spend locked up in little metal boxes – be they trains, planes or cars – the less time we spend face to face with other human beings. Communities are bound to suffer."[20]

Nicholas Faith, in a book on road safety based on a Channel 4 series titled simply *Crash*, highlights the physical dangers of alienation on the roads themselves: "With speed goes aggression, for the driver's mind-set is often that of a soldier in charge of a deadly weapon: the accelerator is the trigger, the steering wheel the sights on the barrel, and because the victims are hidden inside their cars they are, like opposing forces on the battlefield, simply depersonalised enemies." In *Crash*, Dr Steve Stadling, a psychologist with Manchester University's Driver Behaviour Research Group, likens driving on a motorway to flying in formation with complete strangers. "What you need to be able to do is to predict what others are likely to do because the predictability of other drivers is the cornerstone of road safety, and if you're flying in formation with complete strangers at high velocity , well, you're on a wing and a prayer there, aren't you?"[21] At the inquest into the first road fatality in Britain in 1896, the coroner said, "This must never happen again." Since then 25 million people have been killed worldwide, and the toll continues to grow with every day that passes.

John Whitelegg, Professor of Environmental Studies at Liverpool John Moores University and head of the Ecologica consultancy, likens our fascination with the car to a Faustian bargain. "In Marlowe and Goethe the image of a figure determined to increase his power and knowledge at whatever cost is a potent one. Faust's bargain with the devil to sell his soul in return for power and knowledge is a powerful metaphor for the forces that drive human wants and aspirations and for the strength of the inner self to defer any consideration of the final price that must be paid. The story of Faust does, of course, have two endings. In one the final price is paid and Faust is delivered to eternal damnation. In the other he escapes and is reconciled with the Creator. The car can liberate the self-imprisoned soul from its perceived boredom in a limited geographical area. It can confer strong feelings of power, external signs of material wealth, sexual mastery and status. These benefits... are purchased at considerable expense. Consequences range from the destruction of health and community in local neighbourhoods to the destruction of planetary life support systems as a consequence of global warming. The ability to crave and enjoy the benefits and the inability to recognise the severity of the price that has to be paid is Faustian in character."[22]

Your soul for a car? It's a hell of a thought.

12

DAEMONS ARE FOREVER

Noam Chomsky, the theoretical linguist, believes man may be "a kind of lethal mutation". He says, "The species appears in the last flick of an evolutionary eye, and has now achieved the capacity to destroy itself (and much else) by means ranging from weapons of mass destruction to environmental catastrophes. Perhaps it will find ways to contain its destructive impulses, and to address what may be ominous problems." He adds, "A rational Martian spectator might not be sanguine about the prospects."[1]

If we continue travelling down the road to nowhere and if, against all expectations, environmental catastrophe does not result, we know how things will stand vis-a-vis the car by the year 2030. The number of motor vehicles in the world, today around 500 million, will have increased to approximately 2.3 billion – of these 456 million will be in China (Volkswagen is already manufacturing them there). World fuel consumption will be 1.3 billion tonnes. Manufacture of vehicles worldwide will produce 200 billion tonnes of carbon dioxide, and 3.5 billion tonnes of waste matter. Global emissions of various oxides of nitrogen, including nitric oxide, nitrogen dioxide and nitrous oxide, will rise to 35 million tonnes a year – greatly increasing the phenomenon known as summer smog and wreaking havoc on human health and the environment. This rise will take place in spite of any reductions that result from the use of catalytic converters. Road deaths as a result of accidents will rise to 2.5 million annually, injuries to 60 million.[2]

It is worth putting the question again: is this truly progress? We have all seen pictures of the earth taken from space and been told that these have changed the way we think. I think it is fair enough to say it has changed the way some people think. Unfortunately, not the people running the world. Shortly after Rachel Carson published *Silent Spring*, British scientist James Lovelock was working at the Jet Propulsion Laboratory at Pasadena in California when he was shown such a photograph. Lovelock says he saw for the first time "our azure-green planet in all its global beauty" and as a result began formulating the theory he called Gaia, the Greek word for the Earth goddess (the name suggested to him by a neighbour, the author William Golding). Gaia was also known as Ge, from which derive the names of the sciences of geography and geology.

Lovelock described Gaia as "a complex entity involving the Earth's biosphere, atmosphere, oceans and soil; the totality constituting a feedback or cybernetic system which seeks an optimal physical and chemical environment for life on this planet." Or, as he also put it, "The entire range of living matter on Earth, from whales to viruses, from oaks to algae, could be regarded as constituting a single living entity, capable of manipulating the Earth's atmosphere to suit its overall needs and endowed with faculties and powers far beyond those of its constituent parts."[3]

In a new preface to his book, *Gaia – A New Look at Life on Earth*, written in 1995, Lovelock wrote: "When I first started this book twenty years ago the future looked good. There were problems looming with people and the environment but all seemed capable of sensible or scientific solution. Now the prospect is at best doubtful. One of the few certainties about the Earth is that we have changed the atmosphere and the land surface more than it has changed by itself in millions of years. These changes still go on, and ever faster as our numbers grow. Ominously nothing yet seems to have happened more noticeable than the ozone hole over Antarctica. Most politicians believe that all we need is growth and trade and that environmental problems can be fixed technologically.

"This normal human optimism reminds me of a time in London in the Second World War. I had the job of checking the quality of the air in an underground air raid shelter. It was in a disused tube tunnel that ran through the soft mud alongside the River Thames. To my dismay I found that vandals had taken away most of the bolts holding together the steel plates of the tunnel to sell for scrap. It would have taken only a small disturbance to burst the tunnel and flood it. The denizens of the shelter did not seem worried about the possibility of being drowned in mud. They were more frightened by the noisy, but in my judgement, less dangerous war on the surface above them. In a way we are still taking away the bolts of the tunnel and feel confident that what we do is harmless because so far nothing has happened."[4]

And the way the rest of the world thinks – who is to blame for that? I name the guilty man, confident that he cannot sue me: Aristotle. It may seem a little unfair to single out only him, because other Greek thinkers undoubtedly had similar ways of looking at things. It is just that Aristotle was the most brilliant and the one who went down in posterity. Dante called him il maestro di color che sanno, the master of those that know, and we know him as The Philosopher (capital T, capital P). Aristotle's aim was "knowledge and the orderly arrangement of it... There were no mysteries that could not be solved, no secrets that could not eventually be made to reveal themselves... Everything would be examined, defined, compared, and placed in its proper order in an orderly universe."[5] When modern man finally came around to examining and learning from the Greek experience, it was the works of Aristotle that laid the cornerstone for his rationality. They continued to dominate thinking until finally thrown into question by those pictures of the earth taken from outer space, and the 'holistic' viewpoints of very recent times. These say basically that Aristotelian, rational thinkers divorce themselves from the universe and nature, seeking to measure and 'conquer' these phenomena, ignoring the dichotomy that they themselves are part of the equation. To quote Professor David Bohm, a modern physicist, "when we come to examine 'the totality of all that is'... the rules enunciated by Aristotle break down."[6]

In determining the way we look at the earth, Christianity – the dominant Western religion – must surely share with The Philosopher much of the blame for our ecological problems. The creation of mankind is described thus in Genesis: "And God blessed them, and God said to them, 'Be fruitful and multiply, and fill the earth and subdue it; and have dominion over the fish of the sea and over the birds of the air and over every living thing that moves upon the earth.' And God said, 'Behold, I have given you every plant yielding seed which is upon the face of all the earth, and every tree with seed in its fruit; you shall have them for food. And to every beast of the earth, and to every bird of the air, and to everything that creeps on the earth, everything that has the breath of life, I have given every green plant for food.' And it was so."[7](There is a temptation to add, "Yea, even unto extinction.").

The men with power – those who run the multinational companies, those building Volkswagens in China, chemical plants in India, and generally flooding the world with cars and other consumer goods – still heed the Judeo-Christian imperative to "fill the earth and subdue it". In their confused, splintered way, the anarchists of Reclaim the Streets are quite right: the enemy is the whole system, which I suppose can just as well be called 'international capitalism' as anything else. The question is: what do we put in its place? In a vacuum such as the back room of a pub in Finsbury Park or my front room here in Cambridge, it is as easy to dream up idealistic visions of a future society as pessimistic ones. Utopian visions, when put into practice, usually flounder on the frailty of human nature. Pessimistic visions have no appeal whatsoever because, as the old song has it, we have to eliminate the negative and accentuate the positive. So what are we left with? Pragmatism? The same song tells us, "don't mess with Mr. In-Between". Our pragmatic politicians, left, right or centre, are much of a muchness: they certainly have no eye for the long term. And as for the media, the concern there is only for the flavour of month.

In her novel *Memoirs of a Survivor*, Doris Lessing projects the modern social disintegration of our cities into the future, and in the process aptly describes the total helplessness of politicians and the media to truly influence events in any way. They are portrayed as an irrelevance, caught helplessly on the floodtide of events. Lessing writes: "Could there be any real difference when this 'ruling class' used words like justice, fair play, equity, order, or even socialism? – used them, might even have believed in them, or believed in them for a time; but meanwhile everything fell to pieces while still, as always, the administrators lived cushioned against the worst, trying to talk away, wish away, legislate away, the worst – for to admit that it was happening was to admit themselves useless... And yet in a way everybody played a part in this conspiracy that nothing much was happening – or that it was happening, but one day things would go in reverse and hey presto! back we would be in the good old days."[8]

It seems to me that it is just like that vis-a-vis the car and the looming environmental crisis. I'm damned if I know what we can do about it but am sure that Messrs Clinton, Gore, Blair and Prescott have not got the foggiest idea either. They just keep taking the tablets and issuing soundbites concerning the joys coming our way in the shape of the global economy. At the same time there is the rather ominous exhortation that times are changing rapidly (note the implication that they change of their own accord), and we have to keep up with them. Why? There is maybe one small ray of political hope: Lionel Jospin, the French Prime Minister, in his first major speech of the year 2000, denounced "une mondialisation débridée" (unbridled globalisation) and, after talking about environmental concerns, proclaimed, "le monde n'est pas qu'un marché (the world is not just a market)."[9] But even if he is out of step with his so-called allies, what M. Jospin can do about it is another matter – besides, the man is French and refuses to eat British beef!

All of us need to change the way we think, the way we see things but I cannot help feeling it is just a little too late in the day for that. When I met veteran anti-roads campaigner John Tyme, in the course of researching this book, I asked him what he thought were humanity's chances of survival. "Not many," he said sadly. "You see we have the technology to enable us to do almost anything but we don't have the institutions to go with it."[10]

Personally, I think it is more a question of a lack of spiritual insight. These are the words of someone who greatly influenced me when I was the age of the average Donga, protesting against the cutting of Twyford Down: "The problem of man and technics is almost always stated in the wrong way. It is said that humanity has evolved one-sidedly, growing in technical power without any comparable growth in moral integrity, or, as some would prefer to say, without comparable progress in education and rational thinking. Yet the problem is more basic. The root of the matter is the way in which we feel and conceive ourselves as human beings, our sensation of being alive, of individual existence and identity. We suffer from an hallucination, from a false and distorted sensation of our own existence as living organisms. Most of us have the sensation that 'I myself' is a separate centre of feeling and action, living inside and bounded by the physical body – a centre which 'confronts' an 'external' world of people and things, making contact through the senses with a universe both alien and strange. Everyday figures of speech reflect this illusion: 'I came into this world', 'You must face reality', 'The conquest of nature'. This feeling of being lonely and very temporary visitors in the universe is in flat contradiction to everything known about man (and all other living organisms) in the sciences. We do not 'come into' this world; we come out of it, as leaves from a tree. Every individual is an expression of nature, a unique action of the total universe."[11]

I still believe this to be absolutely true. Most people, including of course those in power, or who think they are in power, see only the hallucination. Indeed, it seems to me, a whole civilisation is founded on it. If so, could a species as wilful as mankind ever own up to the fact that it lives a lie? I recognise the difficulty in myself, for while I believe the analysis to be true, I very often am unable to experience, to feel it. Instead I feel apart, alone and afraid. I suppose it all boils down to the fact that – as the magician says – now you see it, now you don't.

Let us get back to the car. One of the most telling arguments I have heard for greater controls on motoring comes from a self-confessed car freak. Lesley Hazleton, motoring correspondent for *Lear* magazine, tells in her book *Confessions of a Fast Woman* of the buzz she experienced driving a Porsche 911: "I'd always thought of cars as mere machinery, but this one made me think of animals – fast, lithe ones like racehorses and panthers. It felt alive beneath my hands, some metal creature bred for wind and speed. At low speed in town, it didn't take much to imagine that it was prancing and snorting, aching for the open road, so I took it to Vermont, and once the highway cleared, I shifted down, ran quickly up to the engine howl of 7,000 rpm, then shifted up into fifth, still accelerating... It ran like the wind. I ran like the wind. It was as though I became the car, or the car became me, and which was which didn't matter anymore... The daemon had emerged, and demanded recognition. Not the demon of medieval imagination, with horns and tail, but the daemon of the ancient Greeks, that pure-burning flame that could take over and hold humans in its grasp, burn them up in its service, inspire them and consume them at the same time..." Hazleton says she is now battling with the daemon. "The daemon clearly still has the upper hand. And although the socially responsible side of me, the side I always thought of as my real self, abhors the effect this has on my mind, the danger I present to others and to myself on the road, the amount of burnt oil I contribute to the pollution of this planet – it is no use. Put me behind the wheel of a fast car and speed takes over. This is not just my personal problem. It is also a political one...

"At the end of the twentieth century, we are still using a one-hundred-year-old technology: the internal-combustion engine. And this basic piece of mechanics pollutes the air so badly that in Los Angeles white air-filters turn black within twenty-four hours, while there are days in Mexico City when people's noses bleed and birds fall dead out of the sky. Yet there is no doubt in my mind that my... delight in speed was intimately bound up with the atavistic qualities of the internal-combustion engine: the vibration and the roar of it, the burning heat, that sense of live metal. And it seems to me that until we can understand the hold of internal combustion over our imaginations and our lives, we cannot achieve a sane balance between our desire for mobility and our desire for a livable planet. One way or the other, we are all in thrall to the daemon."[12]

Once again we return to that Faustian bargain. To take the analogy a step further, let us imagine a scene from the Second Coming of Christ. Remember how he was tempted by the devil the first time around? A scenario for the Second Coming might read something like this:

And the devil pointed to a state-of-the-art Italian sports car and said to him, "Worship me and you can have this baby. She accelerates from 0-100 mph in 10 seconds, achieves 420-horsepower and 186mph. She'll cruise at 140 and you won't feel or hear a thing. She's got overhead cams, triple carbs, double-wishbone suspensions, anti-lock braking and electronic fuel injection. There's cruise and climate control and power steering. The upholstery is the softest calf-skin, the dash rainforest teak and the trim gold-plated. She comes with a built-in six-deck stereo compact disc player with graphic equaliser. There's an on-board computer, phone and fax machine. She'll take you all over the world and when you drive her you will feel incredibly powerful. She is your passport to a life of adventure and glamour. She will make you the envy of everyone you meet and win you any girl you fancy. All you have to do is wave two fingers to your fellow man and the planet in general."

Jesus said, "Get thee behind me, Satan."

So the devil climbed into the back seat and – vroom! – they roared off, running like the very wind itself, the blood pounding in their veins, the adrenaline flowing through their bodies, smiles on their faces and stars in their eyes.

Heading down the road to nowhere.

FOOTNOTES

Introduction
1 AG Pigou, Proceedings of the British Academy, vol 32, page 13.
2 Alexander Pope, 1688-1744.
3 Cambridge County Council Annual Review 1999.
4 Ibid.
5 Ibid.

Future Scenario One
1 Rachel Carson, Silent Spring, Hamish Hamilton, London, 1963.
2 Ibid.
3 John McPhee, Encounters with the Archdruid, 1971.

Chapter One
1 Oxford Illustrated Encyclopedia of Invention and Technology, Oxford University Press, 1992.
2 Ibid.
3 David Sacks, Encyclopedia of the Ancient Greek World, Constable, London, 1997.
4 Pavel Augusta, The Big Book of Transport, Octopus, London 1987.
5 Shorter Oxford English Dictionary, Oxford University Press, 1933.
6 Horace, Epistles II.2.72-5.
7 Florence Dupont, La vie quotidienne du citoyen romain sous la République, Hachette, Paris, 1989.
8 Nicholas Purcell, The life of the city, in The World of Rome, edited by Peter Jones and Keith Sidwell, Cambridge University Press, 1997.
9 Phil Grabsky, I, Caesar – Ruling the Roman Empire, BBC Books, London, 1997.
10 Barbara Preston, The Impact of the Motor Car, Dyfed: Brefi Press, 1991, cited Zuckermann.

11 Oxford Illustrated Encyclopedia of Invention and Technology, Oxford University Press, 1992.

12 Anthony Bird, Roads and Vehicles, Longmans, London 1965.

13 Ivan Sparkes, Stagecoaches & Carriages, Spurbooks, 1975.

14 Tableau de Paris, cited by Zuckermann.

15 Ivan Sparkes, Stagecoaches & Carriages, Spurbooks, 1975.

16 Ibid.

17 Anthony Bird, Roads and Vehicles, Longmans, London 1965.

18 Raymond Flowers and Michael Wynn Jones, One Hundred Years of Motoring – An RAC Social History of the Car, The Royal Automobile Club in association with McGraw Hill, Maidenhead 1981.

19 Anthony Bird, Roads and Vehicles, Longmans, London 1965.

20 Gentleman's Magazine, March 1756, cited by Bird.

21 Oxford Illustrated Encyclopedia of Invention and Technology, Oxford University Press, 1992.

22 The Turnpike Road System in England, William Albert, Cambridge University Press, 1972.

23 Annals of Agriculture, Volume Two, 1786, cited by Bird.

24 Cited by Anthony Bird, Roads and Vehicles, Longmans, London 1965.

25 HB Cresswell, Seventy Years Back, Architectural Review, December 1958.

26 Raymond Flowers and Michael Wynn Jones, One Hundred Years of Motoring – An RAC Social History of the Car, The Royal Automobile Club in association with McGraw Hill, Maidenhead 1981.

27 John Whitelegg, Critical Mass, Pluto Press, London, 1997.

28 Richard Sutton, Motor Mania, Stories from a Motoring Century, Collins & Brown, London, 1996.

Chapter Two

1 Dick Feller, Lord Mister Ford, Valley Music.

2 Alphonse Karr, Les Guèpes, 1849.

3 Jane Austen, Sense and Sensibility, Chatto & Windus, London.

4 Arthur Young, Travels in France, cited by Christopher

Hibbert in The French Revolution, Allen Lane, London 1980.
5 Tableau de Paris, cited by Zuckermann.
6 EJ Hobsbawm, The Age of Revolution, Weidenfeld and Nicolson, London 1962.
7 Raymond Flowers and Michael Wynn Jones, One Hundred Years of Motoring – An RAC Social History of the Car, The Royal Automobile Club in association with McGraw Hill, Maidenhead 1981.
8 Lord Montagu of Beaulieu and F Wilson McComb, Behind the Wheel – The Magic and Manners of Early Motoring, Paddington Press, London 1977.
9 Motoring Through the Years, National Benzole Company Ltd., London, 1969.
10 Flowers and Michael Wynn Jones.
11 CA O'Flaherty (Ed), Transport Planning and Traffic Engineering, Arnold, London, 1997.
12 Shelley Rohde, A Private View of LS Lowry, Collins, London 1979.
13 Richard Sutton, Motor Mania – Stories from a Motoring Century, Collins & Brown, London, 1996.
14 Ibid.
15 Ibid.
16 Pavel Augusta, The Big Book of Transport, Octopus, London 1987.
17 Anthony Bird, Roads and Vehicles, Longmans, London 1965.
18 Flowers and Michael Wynn Jones.
19 Ibid.
20 Anthony Bird, Roads and Vehicles, Longmans, London 1965.
21 Ibid.
22 Ibid.
23 Ibid.
24 Lord Montagu of Beaulieu and F Wilson McComb.
25 Ibid.
26 Flowers and Michael Wynn Jones.
27 Lord Montague of Beaulieu and Patrick Macnaghten, Home James – The Chauffeur in the Golden Age of Motoring, Weidenfeld and Nicolson, London 1982.
28 Lord Montagu of Beaulieu and F Wilson McComb.

29 Lord Montague of Beaulieu and Patrick Macnaghten.
30 M Hamer, Wheels Within Wheels, Routledge and Kegan Paul, London 1987.
31 Sir Osbert Sitwell, Left Hand, Right Hand, London, 1973, cited in by Lord Montagu of Beaulieu and F Wilson McComb.
32 TO Lloyd, Short Oxford History of the Modern World, Empire to Welfare State, Oxford University Press, 1970.
33 Cited by Flowers and Michael Wynn Jones.

Chapter Three
1 Lord Montague of Beaulieu and Patrick Macnaghten, Home James – The Chauffeur in the Golden Age of Motoring, Weidenfeld and Nicolson, London 1982.
2 Rupert Prior, Motoring – The Golden Years, A Pictorial Anthology, Tiger Books, London, 1994.
3 Ibid.
4 The Saturday Book, cited by Charles Owen in The Grand Days of Travel, Webb & Bower, Exeter, 1979.
5 JR Buckley, Cars for the Connoisseur, Batsford, London 1960.
6 Rodney Dale, Halcyon Days – Recollections of Vintage Motoring, Fern House, Haddenham, 1999.
7 Adolf Hitler, Die Grünen im Bundestag, translated by Wolfgang Zuckermann and cited by him in End of the Road.
8 David Henshaw, The Great Railway Conspiracy, Leading Edge, Hawes, North Yorkshire, 1991.
9 Rodney Dale, Halcyon Days – Recollections of Vintage Motoring, Fern House, Haddenham, 1999.
10 Richard Sutton, Motor Mania, Stories from a Motoring Century, Collins and Brown, London, 1960.
11 Interview with author, 1999.
12 Rodney Dale, Halcyon Days – Recollections of Vintage Motoring, Fern House, Haddenham, 1999.
13 Ibid.
14 Richard Sutton, Motor Mania, Stories from a Motoring Century, Collins and Brown, London, 1960.
15 Motoring Through The Years, The National Benzole Company Ltd., London, 1969.
16 Wolfgang Zuckermann, End of the Road, Lutterworth Press, Cambridge 1991.

Chapter Four

1 Wolfgang Zuckermann, End of the Road, Lutterworth Press, Cambridge 1991.

2 Ibid.

3 Bill Bryson, Notes from a Small Island, Doubleday, London, 1995.

4 CA O'Flaherty (Ed), Transport Planning and Traffic Engineering, Arnold, London, 1997.

5 Wolfgang Zuckermann, interview with author, Avignon, 1999.

6 Corelli Barnett, The Audit of War: The Illusion and the Reality of Britain as a Great Power, 1986.

7 Blair Puts the Accent on the North, Daily Mail, December 6, 1999.

8 Lion Television production The Road to Nowhere for BBC2 programme Traffic, 1999.

9 Interview with author, 1999.

10 Ibid.

11 Former motorway worker Brian Behan interviewed in Lion Television production The Road to Nowhere for BBC2 programme Traffic, 1999.

12 Ewan MacColl, Song of a Road, Topic Records, TSCD 802.

13 Suzanne Greaves, Motorway nights with the stars, The Times, August 14 1985.

14 Ibid.

15 David Henshaw, The Great Railway Conspiracy, Leading Edge, Hawes, North Yorkshire, 1991.

16 David Henshaw, interview with author, 1999.

17 Quoted in David Henshaw, The Great Railway Conspiracy, Leading Edge, Hawes, North Yorkshire, 1991.

18 Robert Adley, Out of Steam – The Beeching Years in Hindsight, Patrick Stephens Ltd., Wellingborough, 1990.

19 Kenneth O Morgan, The People's Peace – British History 1945 – 1990, Oxford University Press, 1990.

20 Lion Television production The Road to Nowhere for BBC2 programme Traffic, 1999.

21 Ibid.

22 Interview with author, 1995.

23 Lion Television production The Road to Nowhere for BBC2 programme Traffic, 1999.

24 Ibid.

Chapter Five
1 Lion Television production The Road to Nowhere for BBC2 programme Traffic, 1999.
2 Ibid
3 David Widdicombe QC, from his introduction to John Tyme's book, Motorways versus Democracy, originally published by Macmillan, London, 1978.
4 Ibid.
5 Ibid.
6 Interview with author, 1999.
7 Kenneth O Morgan, The People's Peace – British History 1945-1990, Oxford University Press, 1992.
8 P Rivers, Politics by Pressure, Routledge and Kegan Paul, London, 1974.
9 Lion Television production The Road to Nowhere for BBC2 programme Traffic, 1999.
10 Ibid.
11 The Ecologist, Blueprint for Survival, 1972:15.
12 John Tyme, Motorways versus Democracy, Macmillan, London 1978, later reprinted by the author.
13 Lion Television production The Road to Nowhere for BBC2 programme Traffic, 1999.
14 John Tyme, Motorways versus Democracy, Macmillan, London 1978, later reprinted by the author.
15 Tom Sharpe, Blott on the Landscape, Martin Secker and Warburg, London, 1975.
16 Lion Television production The Road to Nowhere for BBC2 programme Traffic, 1999.
17 Peter Hopewell, Saint Cross – England's Oldest Almshouse, Phillimore, Chichester, 1995.
18 Interview with author, 1999.
19 Barbara Bryant, Twyford Down – roads, campaigning and environmental law, E & FN Spon, London, 1996.

Chapter Six
1 John Cole, As It Seemed To Me – Political Memoirs, Weidenfeld & Nicolson, London 1995.
2 Kenneth O Morgan, The People's Peace – British History

1945-1990, Oxford University Press, 1992.
3 Margaret Thatcher, The Downing Street Years,
HarperCollins, London, 1993.
4 Lion Television production The Road to Nowhere for BBC2
Traffic series, 1999.
5 Mike Robinson, The greening of British party politics,
Manchester University Press, 1992.
6 Hansard.
7 Lion Television production The Road to Nowhere for BBC2
Traffic series, 1999.
8 Ibid.
9 Morton's mountain, Rail Professional magazine, October
1999.
10 Interview with author, 1999.
11 Mike Robinson, The greening of British party politics,
Manchester University Press, 1992.
12 Spike Milligan, If I were... Cecil Parkinson, The Times,
March 10 1990.
13 Interview with author, 1999.
14 Ian Macdonald, Revolution in the Head: the Beatles'
records and the Sixties, Fourth Estate, London, 1994.
15 Lion Television production The Road to Nowhere for
BBC2 Traffic series, 1999.
16 Road Block – How People Power is Wrecking the Roads
Programme, Alarm UK, with the aid of the Goldman
Environmental Foundation, London 1995.

Chapter Seven
1 Evidence to 1987 M3 public inquiry.
2 Robert Lamb, Promising the Earth, Routledge, London,
1996.
3 Interview with author, Basingstoke January 2000.
4 Ibid.
5 Simon Fairlie, Tunnel Vision – The Lessons of Twyford
Down, The Ecologist, Vol 23 No 1, January/February 1993.
6 Interview with author, Basingstoke January 2000.
7 Barbara Bryant, Twyford Down – roads, campaigning and
environmental law, E & FN Spon, London, 1996.
8 Interview with author, Basingstoke January 2000.
9 Barbara Bryant, Twyford Down – roads, campaigning and

environmental law, E & FN Spon, London, 1996.

10 Ibid.

11 Hansard.

12 Barbara Bryant, Twyford Down – roads, campaigning and environmental law, E & FN Spon, London, 1996.

13 Ibid.

14 Ibid.

15 Interview with author, Basingstoke January 2000.

16 Ibid.

17 Simon Fairlie, Tunnel Vision – The Lessons of Twyford Down, The Ecologist, Vol 23 No 1, January/February 1993.

18 Edward Abbey, The Monkey Wrench Gang, Robin Clark, London, 1978.

19 Michael Dynes, The Times, February 28 1992.

20 Derek Wall, Earth First and the Anti-Roads Movement, Routledge, London, 1999.

21 Ibid.

22 Ibid.

23 Ibid.

24 Barbara Bryant, Twyford Down – roads, campaigning and environmental law, E & FN Spon, London, 1996.

25 Ibid.

26 Interview with author, 1999.

27 Derek Wall, Earth First and the Anti-Roads Movement, Routledge, London, 1999.

28 Ibid.

29 Ibid.

30 John Vidal, Twyford showdown on motorway trail, The Guardian, July 5 1993.

31 Derek Wall, Earth First and the Anti-Roads Movement, Routledge, London, 1999.

32 Andrew Rowell, Green Backlash – global subversion of the environment movement, Routledge, London, 1996.

33 John Vidal, The fluffy and the bloody, The Guardian, June 24 1994.

34 Paul Brown, Former EC chief backs Twyford Down protest, The Guardian, August 3 1993.

35 The Ecologist, Vol 23 No. 3, May/June 1993.

Chapter Eight

1 George Walden, Praying for conversion on the road from Whitehall, Daily Telegraph, November 15

2 Mick Brown, When the Dongas meet the bulldozers, Daily Telegraph, September 27 1993.

3 Ibid.

4 Ibid.

5 John Vidal, That dying fall, The Guardian, December 10 1993.

6 Derek Wall, Earth First! and the Anti-Roads Movement, Routledge, London, 1999.

7 Toby Moore, The protesters you could take home to mother, Daily Telegraph May 14 1994.

8 Stephen Venables, High point in the bid to block the roads, Daily Telegraph, July 30 1994.

9 Sandra Barwick, The heart that rules the head, Sunday Telegraph, September 4 1994.

10 Ibid.

11 Wendy Holden, Not in my back yard, protests Bel Mooney, Daily Telegraph, August 6 1994.

12 Lion Television production The Road to Nowhere for BBC2 programme Traffic, 1999.

13 Ibid.

14 Charles Glover and Toby Moore, Time to turn the tide of tarmac, Daily Telegraph, November 8 1993.

15 Ibid.

16 Lion Television production The Road to Nowhere for BBC2 programme Traffic, 1999.

Chapter Nine

1 Adrian Lee, Anti-road warriors prepare for third battle of Newbury, The Times, January 8 1996.

2 Adrian Lee, Roux-trained chef hands the protesters victory on a plate, The Times, January 13 1996.

3 Ibid.

4 Adrian Lee, Bypass protesters claim early win in battle of Newbury, The Times, January 10 1996.

5 Adrian Lee, Bypass work halted on day three as guards are washed out, The Times, January 12 1996.

6 Adrian Lee, Police arrest 34 to break Newbury bypass

deadlock, The Times, January 13 1996.

7 Nigel Williamson and Tim Jones, Newbury protesters face eviction from bypass base, The Times, January 17 1996.

8 Edward Abbey, writing in Ecodefense by David Foreman and B Haywood, Abzug Press, Chico, California, 1993.

9 Edward Abbey, The Monkey Wrench Gang, Robin Clark, London 1991.

10 Stephen Farrell, The naked truth shocks father of anti-car protester, The Times January 19 1996.

11 Adrian Lee, Court backs eviction of bypass protesters, The Times, January 27 1996.

12 Penny Wark, Classes unite for cake and social protest, Sunday Times, January 28 1996.

13 Stephen Farrell, Newbury evictions defeat mountaineer, The Times, March 8 1996.

14 Stephen Farrell and Alexandra Williams, The sheriff of Newbury takes on the treetop greens, The Times, March 11 1996.

15 Newbury activist quoted by Derek Wall in Earth First! and the Anti-Roads Movement, Routledge, London 1999.

Chapter Ten

1 Interview with author, London, December 1999.

2 Derek Wall, Earth First! and the Anti-Roads Movement, Routledge, London 1999.

3 Ibid.

4 Action Update, February 1996.

5 M11 activist Mix quoted by Derek Wall in Earth First! and the Anti-Roads Movement, Routledge, London 1999.

6 "Kev", Reclaim the Streets demonstrator, Cambridge 1999.

7 Tilly, an activist quoted by Wall.

8 David Rennie, Swampy digs for literary victory, Daily Telegraph, June 13 1997.

9 Rachel Sylvester, Bury Swampy in concrete, says Minister, Daily Telegraph, March 15 1997.

10 James Bartholomew, Swampy is bogged down over airport, Daily Telegraph, April 2 1997.

11 Sean O'Neill, Swampy in another hole, Daily Telegraph, June 3 1997.

12 Tom Leonard and Sandra Barwick, I'm proud of him, says

mother of Swampy, Daily Telegraph February 1 1997.

13 Mark Inglefield, Mandrake, Daily Telegraph, August 3 1997.

14 AJ McIlroy, The junior Swampy, Daily Telegraph, August 27 1998.

15 Tom Leonard, Swampy junior is a vandal, say neighbours, Daily Telegraph, August 29 1998.

16 Chat with author, Stockholm 1998.

17 John Jordan, The art of necessity: the subversive imagination of anti-road protest and Reclaim the Streets, DiY Culture – Party & Protest in Nineties Britain, Edited by George McKay, Verso, London, 1998.

18 RTS Agitprop No 1, July 1996.

19 Derek Wall, Earth First! and the Anti-Roads Movement, Routledge, London, 1999.

20 John Jordan, The art of necessity: the subversive imagination of anti-road protest and Reclaim the Streets, DiY Culture – Party & Protest in Nineties Britain, Edited by George McKay, Verso, London, 1998.

21 Ibid.

22 Ibid.

23 Adam Sherwin, Internet message sets off a rampage, The Times, June 19 1999.

24 Protesters 'paid' to riot in City, Sunday Times, June 20, 1999.

25 The Observer, June 20, 1999.

Chapter Eleven

1. Interview with author, Cambridge, June 1999.

2. Ibid.

3. Ibid.

4. James Nadin, Cambridge Weekly News, June 16 1999.

5. Critical Mass website, http://www.critmass.org.uk/em/law.html

Future Scenario Two

1. Based on Arthur C Clarke's forecasts for the future in Predictions, Ed: Sian Griffiths, Oxford University Press, 1999.

2. Wolfgang Zuckermann, End of the Road, Lutterworth Press, Cambridge 1991.

3. Interview with author, London, January 2000.

4. Ibid.

5. Lynn Sloman, A better way to live, Transport Retort, issue 22/4 autumn 1999

6. Ibid.

7. Ibid.

8. Mike Hurst, Teenager leads street campaign, Yorkshire Evening Post, June 17 1999.

9. Bringing home ideas, Transport Retort, issue 22/4 autumn 1999

10. Ibid.

11. David Begg, Walking – a pedestrian strategy for Edinburgh and the Lothians, Lothian Regional Council.

12. Streets for People newsletter, April 1999.

13. Leslie Folkard, British Trams: a pictorial survey, Barton, Truro, 1978.

14. David Henshaw, A to B, 19 West Park, Castle Cary, Somerset BA7 7DB. Tel/fax: 01963 351649.

15. All right, strictly speaking the Swedish is farthinder, all one word, a composite of fart (speed) and hinder (obstacle), Stora svensk-engelska ordboken, Esselte Studium, 1988.

16. Wolfgang Zuckermann, End of the Road, Lutterworth Press, Cambridge 1991.

17. Ibid.

18. Andrew Parker, For three years a woman's body lay here as the world drove past, The Sun, January 7 2000.

19. John Adams, Hypermobility: too much of a good thing, Prospect, 2000.

20. Richard Price, Is Britain now just a hell on wheels? Daily Mail, December 1 1999.

21. Nicholas Faith, Crash – the limits of car safety, Boxtree (in association with Channel 4), London, 1997.

22. John Whitelegg, Critical Mass – Transport, Environment and Society in the Twenty-first Century, Pluto Press, London, 1997.

Chapter Twelve

1 Predictions, Ed: Sian Griffiths, Oxford University Press, 1999.

2 Estimates by team headed by D. Teufel at Heidelberg

Umwelt und Prognose Institut and cited by John Whitelegg in Critical Mass - Transport, Environment and Society in the Twenty-first Century, Pluto Press, London, 1997.

3 James Lovelock, Gaia - A New Look at Life on Earth, Oxford University Press, 1979.

4 James Lovelock, Gaia - A New Look at Life on Earth, Oxford University Press, preface to 1995 edition.

5 Robert Payne, The Triumph of the Greeks - Their History and Culture, Hamish Hamilton, London, 1964.

6 David Bohm, Wholeness and the Implicate Order, Routledge & Kegan Paul, London, 1980.

7 The Bible, Genesis 1.27 - 2.4.

8 Doris Lessing, The Memoirs of a Survivor, The Octagon Press, London, 1974.

9 M Jospin dénonce une "mondialisation débridée", Le Monde, January 4 2000.

10 Interview with author, December 1999.

11 Alan Watts, The Book on the Taboo Against Knowing Who You Are, Jonathan Cape, London, 1969.

12 Lesley Hazleton, Confessions of a Fast Woman, Flamingo, London 1992.